SAINT PHILOMENA
Powerful with God

"The souls of the just are in the hand of God, and the torment of death shall not touch them. In the sight of the unwise they seemed to die: and their departure was taken for misery; and their going away from us for utter destruction: but they are in peace. And though in the sight of men they suffered torments, their hope is full of immortality. Afflicted in few things, in many they shall be well rewarded: because God hath tried them, and found them worthy of Himself. As gold in the furnace He hath proved them, and as a victim of a holocaust He hath received them, and in time there shall be respect had to them. The just shall shine, and shall run to and fro like sparks among the reeds. They shall judge nations and rule over people, and their Lord shall reign for ever."

—Wisdom 3: 1-8

D0051362

Saint Philomena. An artist's conception of the now famous virgin martyr of the Roman era whose tomb was discovered on May 25, 1802 in the Catacomb of St. Priscilla in Rome but about whom there is no historical record.

Saint Philomena
Powerful with God

SISTER MARIE HELENE MOHR, S.C.

REFERENCE LIBRARIAN
SETON HILL COLLEGE
GREENSBURG, PENNSYLVANIA

"*Come, spouse of Christ, receive the crown, which
the Lord hath prepared for thee for ever: for the love
of whom thou didst shed thy blood. Thou hast loved
justice and hated iniquity: therefore God, thy God, hath
anointed thee with the oil of gladness above thy fellows.
With thy comeliness and thy beauty, set out, proceed
prosperously, and reign.*"
     —Tract from the Roman Missal
     Feast of a Virgin Martyr

TAN BOOKS AND PUBLISHERS, INC.
Rockford, Illinois 61105

Nihil Obstat: John A. Schulien, S.T.D.
                   Censor Librorum

Imprimatur: ✠ Moyses E. Kiley
                   Archiepiscopus Milwauchiensis
                   March 9, 1953

ISBN: 0-89555-332-5

Library of Congress Catalog Card No.: 88-50160

Printed and bound in the United States of America.

TAN BOOKS AND PUBLISHERS, INC.
P.O. Box 424
Rockford, Illinois 61105

1988

Dedicated

to

His Excellency, the Most Reverend Hugh L. Lamb
First Bishop of Greensburg

A statue of St. John Vianney, the Curé of Ars (1786-1859), kneeling before a statue of St. Philomena to whom he was especially devoted and to whom he ascribed all the miracles worked at Ars. St. John Vianney was one of the principal original promoters of devotion to St. Philomena.

St. Philomena Today

ST. PHILOMENA'S STORY is unique in the annals of the saints. For here is the story of a virgin and martyr of the Roman era who had remained for centuries unknown to history. Only upon the disinterment of her bones in 1802 did the Catholic world start to learn about her. Then, with the transfer of her relics to a shrine at Mugnano, Italy (near Naples), graces, favors and miracles through her intercession began to abound. Thus did the popularity of this "unknown saint" begin to spread worldwide—with such incredible rapidity and success that in 35 years the Pope (Gregory XVI) named her the "Wonderworker of the 19th Century," officially approved her cultus and raised her to the altar. Thereafter St. Philomena's popularity increased and spread worldwide; to all she became known as "Philomena, Powerful with God."

During the 20th century, St. Philomena's cultus continued to be established everywhere, and national shrines in her honor were erected in Paris, France; in Pinner, England; at Seton Hill in Greensburg, Pennsylvania; and in Briggsville, Wisconsin, to mention the more famous ones.

Devotion to St. Philomena was widespread at the first publishing of this present book in 1952, which was written to commemorate the 150th anniversary of the discovery of her relics. But then on February 14, 1961, just prior to Vatican Council II, St. Philomena's feast was dropped from Church calendars, along with the feasts of a number of other saints and famous events in the lives of Jesus and Mary and the history of the Church. Ever since that time a certain amount of confusion has surrounded devotion to St. Philomena. This action by Rome gave many Catholics the impression that St. Philomena was no longer a saint or that the Church was trying to discourage devotion to her. Neither supposition, however, is correct.

The Instruction of the Sacred Congregation of Rites regarding St. Philomena's feast was a *liturgical* directive, not a denial of saint-hood nor a directive regarding private devotion. The Instruction stated: *Festum autem S. Philumenae V. et M. (11 augusti) e quolibet calendario expungatur*—"But the Feast of St. Philomena, Virgin and Martyr (August 11), should be removed from every calendar whatsoever." (*Acts of the Apostolic See*, March 29, 1961, no. 33).

This Instruction would seem to have had little or no effect in the United States, however, because—as anyone can verify by checking an old missal—a feast of St. Philomena had not been listed in Catholic missals for a number of years—even before the Instruction. There is none listed, for example, in the 1952 missal; a 1937 missal does show a feast of St. Philomena, but it is listed in a special supplement of feasts for the United States, some perhaps to be observed only in certain dioceses. (The Mass to be said was the Common of a Virgin Martyr.) Thus, in the United States the Feast of St. Philomena had apparently ceased being observed years ago (perhaps through the calendar reform of 1913), although probably continuing to be observed in other parts of the world.

Private devotion to St. Philomena, however, had been wide-spread in this country prior to the Instruction, and it is a great loss that in recent years, due to a misunderstanding of the mean-ing of the Instruction from Rome, devotion to St. Philomena has fallen into neglect, thus depriving innumerable souls of the graces and favors that this saint obtains for her supplicants. Queries to the Sacred Congregation of Rites back in 1961 would perhaps have saved several shrines from falling into neglect or even from being dismantled.

For even now it seems that in certain places Mass can still be celebrated in honor of St. Philomena. As explained by Father Giovanni Braschi, the present director of St. Philomena's shrine in Mugnano, Italy and a fervent devotee of the Saint, "She [St. Philomena] can be venerated by means of the external feast and the Mass from the Common of the Martyrs, not only in Mugnano, Italy but also in those places where for local reasons devotion to the Saint exists."

On January 12, 1987, the day on which St. Philomena's oil is annually blessed, Bishop Michele R. Camerlengo of Nola, Italy, the diocese in which Mugnano is located, offered Mass at the Shrine of St. Philomena. This was a double feast: the Feast of the Patronage of St. Philomena and the Feast of the Baptism of Our Lord. In his sermon the Bishop referred to St. Philomena's intercession for us from Heaven, and he explained that, like all the saints, St. Philomena was holy because she listened to Jesus, because she was a docile and attentive disciple of Jesus Christ, the Source of all holiness. He said that the way we truly honor St. Philomena is by following in the path of her holiness (to martyrdom, if need be): the path of obedience to the Father, of love of neighbor, of Gospel perfection, of listening to the Word of God. (A videotape of this Mass and sermon is owned by St. Philomena's Center in the United States.) Thus, the Shrine of St. Philomena in Mugnano, Italy is active today, carrying on devotion to this beloved saint.

Unfortunately, this is not true of several of the other formerly active national shrines. The famous shrine of St. Philomena at St. Gervais in Paris is no longer in operation, nor are those in Pinner, England, or Seton Hill, Greensburg, Pennsylvania, or Briggsville, Wisconsin. (The Briggsville shrine is still in existence, complete with a beautiful statue of the Saint, even though devotions to her are no longer conducted there.)

In 1987 a new shrine of St. Philomena was established in the United States; it is located in Queen of the Angels Church in Dickinson, Texas. In November, 1987 Father Braschi travelled to the United States to visit the Catholic couple responsible for establishing this shrine and for reactivating the Living Rosary, a devotion of which St. Philomena is the patroness. Father Braschi was very pleased with what he found, and he designated these devoted lay people as the National Center of the Confraternity of St. Philomena for the United States and Canada. The address is Mr. & Mrs. Richard Melvin, National Center for St. Philomena, 5013 Harbor Light Drive, Dickinson, Texas 77539.

In a recent booklet Father Braschi writes of a conversation between Pope Paul VI and Msgr. M. Fernandes, the Bishop of Mysore, India and head of St. Philomena's Cathedral there. The Bishop had asked the Pontiff what action he was supposed to take as far as the February 14, 1961 Instruction was concerned. His Holiness gave him this counsel: "Continue as before and don't upset the people."

Anyone who looks up St. Philomena in a Catholic reference book may find evidence of controversy and even some disparaging remarks about her. This is not a new development. The early 20th century saw much archaeological discussion and controversy regarding St. Philomena's relics, with two of the main protagonists being Professor Marucchi and Father G. Bonavenia, S.J. Professor Marucchi disputed the authenticity of the relics found in the famous tomb in 1802, arguing (in 1904 and 1906) that the disarrangement of the name tiles on the tomb (cf. pp. 6 and 11 - 12 of this book) indicated that the tiles and the tomb had been re-used and that the bones which had been found there were not those of Philomena but of some unknown maiden. Father Bonavenia (writing in 1906 and 1907) responded to Professor Marucchi in two essays, concluding that the bones discovered *were indeed* those of St. Philomena. The Abbé Francis Trochu, famous for his biography of the Curé of Ars (a great devotee of St. Philomena), also published a monograph (*La "petite Sainte" du Curé d'Ars*, 1924) defending the historicity of the martyr. Much other material was also written on the question as well.

Father Braschi reports that two recent archaeologists have concurred with Father Bonavenia in rejecting Professor Marucchi's thesis; they are Prandi and Mistillo, writing in the book *Graffiti di S. Pietro*, I, p. 501, dated and signed: "Rome, Nov. 29, 1963." Father Braschi concludes: "Finally, the historian Georg. Markhof, in his report on the book *Filomena: The Uncomfortable Miracle*

(Vienna, 1981), expresses himself against Marucchi as follows: 'I consider the Italian archaeologist Marucchi's view to be superficial and marked by malice—which is very surprising when one considers his excellent reputation. Evidently he had been biased against St. Philomena, and not disposed—as would have been sufficient for a scientist—to look into the case objectively.'"

Nonetheless, Marucchi's opinion is still found surfacing in various reference book articles on St. Philomena. Therefore the reader should be alerted to the background of the controversy, that he might not unwittingly accept Marucchi's theory as undisputed fact. As often happens in speculation, pure hypotheses soon gain increasing credence the more they are repeated, especially when repeated in print. But it takes little reflection to realize that a wrong notion is still wrong, no matter how many times repeated—and even if put into print.

Also, with regard to articles in reference books, one should realize that there exists a certain stylistic device—common to most popular journalists today—which consists of always proposing an opposite view to every position stated, no matter how correct the position may be nor how absurd or groundless its opposite—all with the idea of letting the reader see "both sides" of the question and decide for himself. Often, nothing is of less service to the truth than such a journalistic stance, for in this approach the writer demonstrates that he has neither searched out the truth for himself nor is he concerned with conveying it to his reader.

In the final analysis, however, and archaeological disputes aside, if St. Philomena is truly in Heaven and worthy of our veneration—and the Popes have said she is—then the faithful are entirely warranted in their devotion to her. Truly, St. Philomena's popularity would scarcely have circulated throughout the world had not those who *are* devoted to her received signal favors in response to their prayers to her for help. (Just try to convince her devotees that she is *not* a saint!) For if she is a saint, she is a saint; and if she is "powerful with God," she is powerful with God. And there is nothing we can do at this late date in history to contravene the facts. All the skeptics saying she is not these things will never diminish her glory if she is. And all the great body of the faithful successfully invoking her intercession will only increase her popularity, until all skepticism is silenced and the will of God to magnify this martyred virgin spouse of His Son is accomplished in the hearts of true believers everywhere.

St. Philomena, Powerful with God, pray for us!

TAN Books and Publishers, Inc.
February 8, 1988

Acknowledgment

THE PRESENTATION of another story of the girl Philomena is, perhaps, only the turning-over for another harvest a field already worked. But a promise made should be kept. In gratitude to St. Philomena for her constant help, this record of her is submitted after two years of research.

Material from other sources has been enriched by direct communication with the Sanctuary of St. Philomena, located in Mugnano del Cardinale, Avelino, Naples.

The Redemptorist Fathers in Pittsburgh made accessible the archives of their American foundation at the first St. Philomena's Church in the new world. These data are exceptionally precious because they record what seems to be St. Philomena's power to restore peace among discordant nationalities.

Father Virgil Roseborough, O.S.B., placed within reading range a wealth of material from St. Vincent Archabbey, Latrobe, Pennsylvania. The catalogue of the *British Museum,* the *Bibliotheque Nationale,* the *Acta Sanctorum,* and the *Enciclopedia Cattolica* proved useful.

Katherine Burton most graciously granted permission to use material from her biography of Pauline Jaricot.

The Anthonian Press, Dublin, readily permitted quoting from the Cecily Hallack story of St. Philomena.

Father Paul O'Sullivan, Dominican author of several books, contributed a letter from a woman in Lisbon recently cured through the intercession of St. Philomena. His book telling of his visit to St. Philomena's shrine was also used.

Sheed and Ward, Inc., obligingly gave the credit line for a

quotation from Bruce Marshall's chapter on the Curé of Ars in *Saints for Now*. Mr. Frank Sheed's translation of Ghéon's *Secrets of the Saints* strengthened other findings.

Father Goodman's 1931 edition of *Saint Philomena* came to light through the courtesy of Pellegrini Company in Australia.

The Library of Congress lent its one holding, entitled *The Life and Miracles of Saint Philomena, Virgin and Martyr*. Though dated 1865, this English translation is from the 1834 French abridgment of the Italian memoirs of Francesco di Lucia.

Actual source material is now at Seton Hill, thanks to Reverend Vincent Giovinetti, pastor of Madonna del Castelo Church, Swissvale, Pennsylvania. It came direct from the Giovinetti family library in Naples and is the original work of Don Francesco di Lucia, the priest who transported the sacred remains of the virgin-martyr, Philomena, from Rome to Mugnano in 1805. This book, entitled *Relazione Istorica della Traslazione del Sacro Corpo e Miracoli di Santa Filomena, Vergine e Martire, da Roma a Mugnano del Cardinale,* is the third edition, dated 1829. From this same collection came the "Annals of Saint Philomena, 1850–1855."

These Italian sources were consulted with the help of Sister Serafina Mazza, S.C., of the department of Italian, Seton Hill College.

To Father Timothy O'Keefe of Wisconsin Dells thanks are extended, and to Father Ignatius Wiltzius of Briggsville sincere appreciation for the unforgettable pilgrimage to the Shrine of St. Philomena.

The story is presented in commemoration of the one hundred and fiftieth anniversary of the finding of St. Philomena's relics, May 24, 1802.

SISTER MARIE HELENE MOHR, S.C.

Contents

A map showing the location of Mugnano, Italy, home of the shrine of St. Philomena. On the lower left is the Bay of Naples. Naples itself is just off the map on the left. (See the road marked "Per Napoli.")

SAINT PHILOMENA
Powerful with God

"Then shall the just stand with great constancy against those that have afflicted them and taken away their labours. These seeing it, shall be troubled with terrible fear, and shall be amazed at the suddenness of their unexpected salvation, saying within themselves, repenting, and groaning for anguish of spirit: These are they whom we had some time in derision and for a parable of reproach. We fools esteemed their life madness and their end without honour; behold, how they are numbered among the children of God, and their lot is among the saints."

—Wisdom 5: 1-5

Sketches of the original tiles found marking St. Philomena's tomb. These sketches are taken from the Italian book *Santa Filomena* (1985) by Fr. Giovanni Braschi, rector of the Shrine Church of St. Philomena in Mugnano, Italy. The upper sketch depicts the position of the tiles as they were found marking St. Philomena's tomb. They read LUMENA PAXTE CUMFI, which makes no sense. The lower sketch shows the order in which they obviously should be; by placing the first tile last, we read PAXTE CUMFI LUMENA. Separating the words properly gives the very intelligible *Pax tecum Filumena*, which, translated from the Latin, is "Peace be with you, Philomena." The original tiles are kept in the Shrine Church at Mugnano.

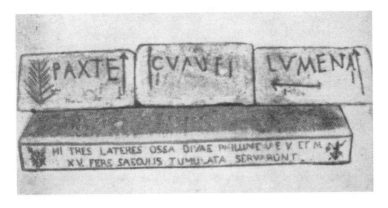

CHAPTER I

Discovery

THE DATE IS 1802. Napoleon, the Corsican adventurer, is fighting his way straight up from the mob, pointing a sword at every monarchical head. Philomena, the celestial adventuress, is rising from the catacombs, waving the palm branch of peace for troubled hearts.

The military strategist, drunk with success, has unbecomingly straddled his power by overlording the Pope, Pius VII. That gentle though courageous "Pontiff of Concordats" sees the need of a spiritual revival. Nineteenth-century Europe, twisted with false complacency, bewildered by political realism, is riding for a fall. It would throw its own fate into the saddle, unless its rocky-horse tactics come to a halt.

Heaven sounds the keynote. Out from God's army of saints marches a teen-aged girl. For more than a thousand years she has been in the reserve corps, awaiting the bugle call. With the serenity of a virgin, and the dignity of a crowned head, Philomena, "Princess of Paradise," brings reinforcements for body and soul. Just where to encamp for concerted action? And when to serve? God knows.

In the month of May, on the twenty-fourth day, Our Lady, Help of Christians, intervenes. Philomena with her lovely winsome ways, her sparkle, her youth, has come to attract!

In a tufa pit in an underground cemetery dedicated to the family of Priscilla, underneath the soil on the road that goes out of the Porta Salaria from Rome to Ancona, excavators are clearing away fallen sand. In the tunnel of soft stone the sharp ring of a pick is heard as it hits a cemented surface. Conscious of his obligation, the excavator stops to investigate with his lamp. A shelf tomb!

His fellow workers gather excitedly to search for some clue to the loculus, since no evidence of violation is visible. Most remarkable! These men had heard that all relics had been removed from this cemetery way back in the sixteenth century. And here is a chamber in good order, solidly walled up with three terra-cotta tiles! Only the very high nobility and celebrated martyrs were placed in marble coffins and then sealed in wall niches. This "find" certainly would make the headlines! This news! Moreover, the singularity of the three marble slabs joined to form the inscription!

With due formality the chief fossor informs the Guardian of Cemeteries. He orders immediate cessation of work. The Monsignor slates the very next day for the public opening of the sarcophagus.

The burial stone was distinguished by several symbols bearing allusion to virginity and martyrdom. This ornamentation had been executed with peculiar force and expression. The instruments of martyrdom seemed to be genuine, and corresponded with sufficient exactness to the revelations of the Saint, recorded at a later date by three persons unknown to one another and in widely separated districts.[1]

The symbols themselves suggest some meanings. Apparently, the virgin, Philomena, whose virginity is shown by a lily, was pierced, struck with arrows, fastened to an anchor, and thrown into the river. Indeed a martyr!

Students of Christian symbols generally agree on the interpretation of these figures on the stone. The emblems breathe the language of faith and hope.

In the anchor there is a resemblance to the cross, the sign of faith in Christ. In both Greek and Roman antiquity there is mention of the sacred anchor. The anchor also connotes hope, refuge, and preservation of life. In the legend of the martyred Philomena there is a passage about the Roman emperor's wrath

[1] These revelations are reprinted in Chapter XII of this book, pages 120–128.

when the anchor he had fastened to the girl's neck wedged in the mud of the Tiber where it still lies. Instead of causing the maiden and her memory to perish, as the sadist planned, the anchor saved her by sinking itself, after angels cut the cord and brought Philomena back to shore, unharmed. Onlookers who witnessed the breaking of the anchor's cord as the virgin was cast into the water saw in this a miracle.

Other saints, including Pope Clement, suffered martyrdom by having an anchor tied to the neck and being dropped into the sea. Emperor Trajan as well as Diocletian decreed this form of brutality.

The two arrows pointing in opposite directions signify torment similar to that which Diocletian exercised on St. Sebastian, the generous tribune of the first cohort. The revealed narratives describe this form of torture as endured by Philomena:

The enraged emperor commanded his executioners to drag the virgin through the streets of Rome, and then shoot at her with arrows. She would not die, and they returned her to prison, to be hauled out again next day for the same treatment. This time the arrows themselves refused to fly. The emperor stormed and called on fire to break this magic. Arrows were made red hot in a fiery furnace and shot at her, but the arrows turned backward and killed six of the bowmen. Only a few shafts pierced the girl. She swooned, and not another archer bent his bow. This evidence of sanctity infuriated the despairing beast in the emperor. He accused Philomena of witchcraft and had her bound to a pole in the dungeon, where again he approached her with jeering love. Each time she repulsed him the cruelty of the madman devised more horrible suffering. He would have her lanced, and he did, thus releasing her pure soul.

The symbols on this newly discovered tomb were crossed by the transverse line of an inscription, painted in vermilion, which still retains its bright red. The first and last letters appear to have been effaced by the instruments of the workmen while endeavoring to detach the slabs from the tomb. But the three slabs make part of only one epigraph:

LUMENA PAXTE CUM FI

A learned Jesuit, Father Parthenion, of the early nineteenth century, thinks the last two letters, *FI*, should be united to the first word of the inscription, according to the usage of the ancient Chaldeans, Phoenicians, Arabs, and Hebrews. The Greeks used it on the burial stones of Christian martyrs. This is noted especially on first-century tombs.

It is quite understandable that these terra-cotta slabs could have been jumbled in the hurried burial imperative upon the merciful hands that laid away martyred bodies in those days of persecution. If the unusual and remarkable epitaph had not been drawn on the spot, the mason who cemented the tiles may have been unaware of the inversion. Correctly arranged the inscription would read: *PAX TECUM FILUMENA* — "Peace be to you, Philomena!"

When possible, artists or engravers marked the slab that instantly sealed the wall niche in the underground city of the dead. If neither craftsman was available, the sexton chiseled an inscription, symbolic of the person interred. A palm branch, a dove, a lily, an anchor, or some other very specific emblem would be used for identification. The name of the martyr was added, if there was certainty.

Representatives of the hierarchy, doctors and surgeons, archaeologists and scientists, city officials and legal administrators, news gatherers, and curious onlookers — breathlessly they assembled at the appointed place, May 25, 1802, to see the lid of the sarcophagus removed.

For hours the milling crowd talked excitedly, pushing close up for full view. Guards sweated in the Italian sun while the people, charged with something beyond their understanding, went completely out of bounds. *The day before a wall tomb had been discovered. An engraved vault. Who?* Nineteenth-century men and women wanted to see for themselves. Churchmen furrowed their brows in serious reflection; some in reasoned doubt.

Then came the stupendous moment. The authorized appointees began the prosecuting investigations. With formal procedure the devices accompanying the inscription were minutely scrutinized. Everything was there to proclaim it the resting place of a martyr. There for all to witness on the slabs were anchor, arrows, and palm. To some it seemed a mystic lily. Or a virgin's lamp, like the parable light.

It is scarcely possible to overestimate the profound reverence that silenced the bystanders and assistants when Monsignor Filippo Ludovici, the keeper of the holy relics, disclosed the precious remains of a young girl!

Physicians examined the skeleton — its small unbroken bones, fractured skull, eye sockets. The maiden had been lanced. Surgeons ascertained the type of wounds inflicted. The experts convened to give a decision stated that the girl had been martyred in her tender youth, at twelve or thirteen years of age.

As early as 1668 the Congregation of Indulgences and Relics had decided that the genuineness of a true relic of a martyr hinged somewhat on the finding of the vial or vase filled with the martyr's blood. The same congregation renewed the decision in 1863.[2]

Astonishing was the enthusiasm of the early Christians for those who were brave enough to die for their faith. Relatives and friends felt comforted by the mere privilege of interring the precious corpse in the family cemetery. Here they marked the slab of stone with the sign of a palm. In the fresh mortar at the side of the grave they placed a small vase containing the martyr's blood.

These vases, called ampullae, having been in a manner consecrated by the blood of martyrs, when later removed from the original place of security, were transferred to the Relic Office in Rome for preservation. There a large collection of these vials of the blood of saints may be venerated on Thursday of Passion Week every year.

[2] Joseph Cardinal Hergenroether, *Primitive Christianity and the Catholic Church* (New York: F. Pustet & Co., 1883), pp. 56–57 et al.

The Roman ampulla resembles a flask of glass or earthenware, having a more or less globular body, and usually two handles.

Not to be confused with the vase of sacred blood is the small receptacle of aromatic spices, placed near the vault. A sense of decency in the Roman Christian inspired him to purify the heavy atmosphere of the catacombs just as we deodorize the funeral parlor today. This was not religious ceremony; nor was it incense-burning. It was simple disinfecting.

This detailed account of the blood ampulla is stressed because of the importance attached to it in the early days of Christianity. Both it and the palm seemed to be certain signs of authenticity.

Embedded in the concrete of the tomb, near the girl's head, was the telltale vial, a slightly broken small vase, containing in dried form a darkish red or brown substance. Scientific testing determined this congealed mass in the vial to be dried blood.

While experts were examining the traces that adhered to the broken vase, as they forced it from its wedged position in the cement, they were startled by a strange chemical reaction. As the small particles were carefully detached and transferred to a clean new vase of clear visibility, glorious shining gems appeared. Precious stones with the luster of purest silver and gold!

The Court of Inquiry was awed. Onlookers gazed reverently and wonderingly on that holy phenomenon. They blessed God. Only theologians understood. Yes, a divine power could and would permit this guarantee of sainthood. There was no question.

The witnesses of the prodigy that day were not men to doubt what their eyes saw. In the century and a half since, scientists have carefully examined the miraculous substance of this same blood. Their testing has proved that the blood concealed in the burial place with her bones is real blood.

The chemical change of the blood convinced the Church dignitaries that a new star had arisen among the blessed. Cardinal Ruffo Scilla, who renewed the seals on the new reliquary after the blood of the Saint had been safeguarded in the crystal vial, deposed in the authentication: "And we have seen her blood changed into several brilliant little precious stones of various colors; also into gold and silver."[3]

Forty-five years later there is striking evidence from the renowned cardinal, Victor Auguste Dechamps. Though a Liberal in youth, Victor, the brother of the Belgian statesman, Dechamps, entered the Redemptorist Order and became an Ultramontane leader. In 1865 he was made Bishop of Namur. In two years he was raised to the Archbishopric of Mechlin, and in 1875 he received the cardinal's hat. As a pulpit orator he attracted international fame, especially while he presided over Malines.

This famous man while he was still a Redemptorist had high regard for Philomena the Saint. As early as 1847 he first witnessed the miracle of the blood in the reliquary at the shrine of Mugnano. In a written statement he testifies: "Need I tell you with what happiness I saw . . . the phial of blood, of that precious blood shed for love of virginity, and for the virginity of love. . . . It is a thing marvelous to see. . . . I had read of it in descriptions, but now I have seen it with my own eyes."[4]

Father Paul O'Sullivan, an active Dominican priest in Lisbon, writes of his experience at the shrine, where he made a novena in 1909. In friendly correspondence, as well as in his book on St. Philomena, Father O'Sullivan speaks freely of his convictions regarding the miracle of her blood. He has written:

"I had the happiness of examining this priceless treasure as many as thirty or forty times. Each time without fail I saw the blood change most marvelously and the transformation was so clear and distinct as not to allow room for the smallest doubt or misconception. Precious stones, rubies and emeralds, pieces of gold and particles of silver appeared mingled with the blood.

[3] Cecily Hallack, *Saint Philomena, Virgin, Martyr, and Wonder-Worker* (Dublin: Anthonian Press, 1936), pp. 53–54.
[4] *Ibid.*, p. 54.

One might shake the reliquary and again the precious stones appeared, not always in the same way but still clearly and distinctly."[5]

This prominent priest continues in his discourse on St. Philomena by citing instances when black particles seemed to replace the gems. More than one person has been forewarned and perhaps encouraged by this to pray for strength to cross life's bridge. It is said these black stones presaged for the Holy Father, Pius IX, the tribulations to be expected during the three decades of his pontificate. This great ruler of the Church expressed his love for the virgin Philomena by his public veneration at her shrine, in royal procession with the ruling King and Queen of Naples and the seven princesses and prince.

From the caretakers of the sanctuary, Sisters of Charity of St. Vincent de Paul, we have up-to-the-minute facts. They say the normal state of the Saint's blood in the clear glass vase is brownish gray somewhat like ashes, but that sometimes brilliant jewels appear. Rubies may outsparkle the emeralds, or the emeralds may outshine the rubies. This rainbow glory takes on richer and richer glow until the sun itself seems to burst in it.

Only once has the substance of the blood disappeared. The horrified pilgrims at the shrine realized only too late that one visitor, an apostate, had come to sneer. His mockery turned to terror and he hurried away. The blood of the Saint reappeared. Several days later the unworthy minister of the Church died at a dinner party, apparently unrepentant!

Marvelous though it seemed to those who witnessed the first miraculous occurrence of the blood that day when the sacred remains of the slain girl were extracted from the tomb in the Priscillian catacomb, there was no hasty action on the part of the Catholic Church. Instead only the wise slowness and circumspection of the Court of Rome. When called upon to pronounce on these extraordinary events, the Ecclesiastical Court

[5] Paul O'Sullivan, O.P. (E.D.M. pseud.), *Saint Philomena the Wonder-Worker*, 4th ed. (Lisbon: The Dominican Press, 1947), p. 42.

began the juridical search. No data were available. It seemed impossible to establish a legal status for a Roman martyr named *Filumena*.

Scientists and archaeologists judged the tomb had been designed in the second or third century. From its position, one specialist set the date at about A.D. 160. Others ranged the possibility up to the Diocletian Age.

Undoubtedly the drawings on the slabs and the bright redness of the paint pointed to the period of the early Christian persecutions. Lettering on the stone is not cut in, but simply painted in a vivid red, like several other stones in that part of the cemetery.

The crust on the lettering suggests that perhaps the color was tempered in the blood of the martyred girl. Some scholars, disregarding the crust, declare the red coloring to be made of red lead, or of cinnabar.[6]

In this particular instance perhaps the slabs were painted while the little maiden's body was being purified from dust and blood, before she was embalmed and wrapped in clean white linen.

The explanation proposed by later investigators of a loculus closed in the dark is unfounded. A fossor, or excavator, no more than a foreman in a mine, would venture into a tomb without his lamp. If this were wanting, or was blown out by flying sand, he would get another lamp.

The cynic will continue his argument that a stone mason could not be guilty of such crass ignorance as the inversion of the slabs. Moreover, the skeptic will insist that a workman who bungled his workmanship would be requested or obliged to rearrange the tiles, in the order required by the reading. Or he will point out that only after the etching is completed and the limestone placed around, does the painter trace the characters. When a single slab walls a vault the etcher executes the design

---

[6] Don Francesco di Lucia, *Relazione Istorica della Traslazione del Sacro Corpo e Miracoli di Santa Filomena, Vergine e Martire, da Roma a Mugnano del Cardinale*, Terza ed. (Napoli: Dai Torchi Di Saverio Giordano, 1829), p. 35.

previously, because the thinness of the slab would not withstand the engraver's hammer after being set in place with a clamp upon the tomb.

Did the fossor jumble the text intentionally because the enclosure really was a Grecian princess, whose royal family would claim the sarcophagus at a later date when the emperor's wrath had subsided? If this be the solution, then why was their beloved child unclaimed for seventeen hundred years? May the answer be that the girl's parents were spirited away to avenge the anger of Diocletian?

The tombstone that originally marked the grave of Philomena tantalized all who read it. Temporarily it was preserved in a Jesuit college along with other ancient inscriptions of martyrs. There both Don Bartolomeo and Don Francesco had seen it, not realizing what importance they would both attach to it in years to come. To these good priests it was just another undeciphered gravestone.[7]

Eventually by order of Pius VII, with the advice of scholars, these terra-cotta slabs were transferred to the Treasury of the Rare Collection of Christian Antiquity in the Vatican.[8] Monsignor Joseph Kirsch, writing about St. Philomena, says the three tiles that closed her tomb were given to the Church of Our Lady of Grace by Leo XII in 1827. That seems to be an appropriate place for them, since our Lady has given refuge to Philomena's sacred remains from the moment of their translation to Mugnano in 1805. Today these precious slabs lie in a case of metal and glass on the opposite side of the nave where the Saint is enshrined.[9] In spirit the reader may visit this sanctuary before this story ends. Now just a peek through the glass reveals the words in their bright, clear redness — *LUMENA PAXTE CUM FI.*

Baffling words! They say so much but tell so little. Was the girl to whom they refer Roman? Or was she a patrician daugh-

[7] Don Francesco, p. 33.

[8] Joseph P. Kirsch, "Saint Philomena," *Catholic Encyclopedia* (New York: The Encyclopedia Press, 1914), Vol. 12, p. 25.

[9] See letter from the Shrine of Mugnano, reprinted in Chapter XII, pages 135–136.

ter of a Grecian house? And was she Philomena? The custodians of the Priscillian catacomb, and the archaeologists who made investigation, Northcote and Marucchi and De Rossi and other researchers in stone, pondered and talked and argued but failed to reach a conclusion. While men were digging for data, Philomena was stepping higher and higher. In thirty-five years after the discovery of her tomb, she would reach the heights of sanctity!

It is to be understood that the scientific examining was not all the work of one day. The immediate lifting from the catacomb was the first step in the official procedure. After the sarcophagus was raised above ground, every detail demanded exactitude. The transferring of the sacred skeleton from its ancient resting place to the silken repository and its encasement in a new wooden box was merely a preliminary move.

Most reverently the clean vial of blood was deposited in a silk-lined ebony casket with the sacred bones, the skull, and the ashes. The case was then locked and triple-sealed by Monsignor Ludovici. Under Guard of Honor the ebony casket was solemnly conveyed to the Custodia of the Cardinal Vicar, a chapel for the bodies of saints.

There in the holy mortuary the precious treasures are protected, awaiting disposition. Only the Supreme Pontiff may delegate orders for bestowal of a relic once it has been consigned to the Custodia Generale. To this treasure house of the Catholic Church bishops must always go in person to beg a relic of the saint they wish to honor in their diocese.

With every relic transferred to the Treasury of the Church a signed document must be submitted. This affidavit bears the signature of theologians, physicians, experts in physical and biological science, representatives of civil as well as ecclesiastical law.

Strange, strange world! The young girl, so revered for her heroism, was soon forgotten. The loculus, that held her body, sealed within its stony silence all memories of her and her loved ones. Records of her family had completely vanished. No trace of a girl named *Filumena* existed in Rome.

The fact that she had rested in Priscilla's ground set a stamp of higher approval. This catacomb is remarkable for its unusual paintings. According to Northcote, an authority on the holy underground, the earliest representation of the Virgin Mother and Child adorns its walls. The second-century painting and that of the Last Supper in which the Apostles are wearing wreaths have added to the admiration that surrounds early saints.

In this same catacomb were discovered the remains of a small basilica built by Pope Sylvester in which he and four other popes were buried.

The name Priscilla is contemporary with that of the Apostles. She is the wife of Aquila, a pupil of St. Paul. Early authorities are inclined to think she is the Priscilla or Prisca from whose home St. Paul sent a greeting in his Epistle to the Romans.

The name Priscilla appears also in the senatorial family of Acilii Glabriones whose burial place was in the catacomb of St. Priscilla on the Via Salaria, in the same plot that rested the precious bones of Philomena.

Yes, Philomena must have lineage that can be proved or associated with the distinguished of her day. The pall of classic training had so stifled the scholarly Roman mind of 1800, it did not try to imagine further just who Philomena might be. The busy world went its way, and remembered not its "dream girl" asleep on her satiny ebony couch.

CHAPTER II

Recognition

THE GREAT DAY FOR PHILOMENA CAME. The patience of a saint was to be rewarded with the incense of glory. And the cause was a poor young priest from the diocese of Nola in Italy. His parish church dedicated to Santa Maria della Grazie was located in Mugnano, a town set amid lively gardens, snuggled in the hills, twenty miles north of Naples.

To the gay Neapolitans, a Virgin-Saint would lend her sweet reserve, her simplicity, and the artistry of her charm. To these dramatic, stormy, fun-loving people Philomena would sparkle with a heavenly glow.

"She came into Byron's Italy, into the Europe of George Sand and Balzac, and preached virginity, the honor due to it, and its glories. She came, a realist among the romantics, pointing out that adventure was the privilege of man's will, not of his body."[10]

Why did Philomena come to Naples? Not for the reason Goethe came. He went because its loveliness relaxed his mind, wearied by international fame. Philomena chose Neapolitans to share with her a name that would someday circle the world. Determined to win the hearts of the gay, she must first win her way with the Roman Curia.

The terrific sweep of action that floodlights Philomena is her own dynamic power from God. The human dynamo that transmitted the power of Philomena to the early nineteenth century was a priest from Mugnano.

[10] Hallack, p. 77.

But first, another clergyman enters the story of the rise of Philomena. He is the illustrious scholar and theologian, Don Bartolomeo di Cesare. Recently appointed Bishop-elect of Potenza, a diocese pleasantly situated about 3000 feet above the valley of the Basento, he meditates. His consecration is scheduled for mid-June. But just today he has received from King Ferdinand IV of Naples a royal commission that will speed up his plans a month.

This Bourbon, third son of Charles III of Spain, has delegated Don di Cesare to represent the royal family at the homecoming of Pius VII who is about to return to Rome after his sojourn in France, where he had gone presumably to crown the Emperor, Napoleon Bonaparte.

At the request of his King, the Neapolitan ecclesiastic prepares to leave Naples about the first of May. Mindful of a recent visit from his young friend, Francesco di Lucia, the older priest invites Francesco to accompany him to Rome as his secretary. The journey by carriage takes three days. They arrive in the Holy City, May 4, 1805.[11]

During the journey they exchange confidence. The experienced prelate understands the problems facing the humble priest from Mugnano. The youth of that parish seem to be dashing headlong into the abyss of unbelief. The revolutionary ideas that strafe the French Empire will scorch Naples soon.

Don Francesco tells that, after praying for guidance, he is inspired to obtain for his domestic chapel the body of a known saint. He longs to have a relic of a virgin-martyr, to encourage young girls to pattern their lives on noble womanhood. He reasons that good wives will set good example. Then parents will rear their children the right way.

The older clergyman encourages his companion and promises to support the petition to the Treasure House of Relics while in Rome. Don Bartolomeo hopes that the request will be granted, though he realizes the young priest is asking a favor beyond his influence to obtain and out of ordinary propriety.

[11] Don Francesco, p. 8.

The scholarly new bishop was a welcome guest at the Vatican. Apart from his diplomatic mission, he cheered the saddened Pope by enthusiastic plans for his recently assigned diocese of Potenza. As the visitor relayed the legend of the "sparkling fountain," a fantastic name given to the sulphur springs of Potenza, even the papal mind could turn to a world of fancy and imagination. We can almost hear the laughter when Bartolomeo told of the romantic deeds of the Carthusian monastery on the Padula Road, not forgetting the famous Potenza omelet, made with a thousand eggs, the offering of the Abbott of San Lorenze to Charles V when that emperor visited the monastery in 1535.

Don Francesco records in memoirs that his friend, the Bishop, remembered the promise concerning the desired relic. About the middle of May, Don Francesco was taken to the Treasure House of Relics, which was under the care of a worthy guardian, Monsignor Don Giacinto Ponzetti,[12] to whom he was presented in the name of the influential Bishop of Potenza.

Only three of the thirteen bodies resting in the sacred place had names. Don Francesco reasoned that nobody is interested in a nameless saint. His choice went immediately to the Girl Saint with the lovely name, Philomena. Hers was the last relic shown to him and it was sealed in an ebony case. The young priest immediately sensed the preciousness of this Virgin-Martyr. Emotion of unforgettable quality burned him with a craving for this girl. Her youthful heroism was exactly the inspiration the young people in Mugnano needed. Her virginal strength would challenge them to purity. This is how Don Francesco describes his feelings at the time:

"Upon seeing the relic of Saint Philomena an invisible force agitated me internally and externally. Then I felt an unusual and intense joy in my heart, and I was filled with a pure desire to possess her sacred body. This was so evident in my countenance that even the custodian of the Treasury became aware of it. . . .

[12] *Ibid.*, p. 15.

"In the case with Saint Philomena's relics there was also a paper containing a copy of the sepulchral inscription, giving her name and the kind of martyrdom she suffered. The particular sweetness and gentleness of the name, Philomena; the Greek and the Latin erudition associated with the name in story and in poetry; the uniqueness of the name; the fact that she was the only girl-martyr there — these and similar thoughts made me long even more for the coveted prize. . . .

"Upon seeing the vase containing her blood, which preached a silent sermon on her courage, her sacrifice, and her triumph, my determination overpowered me. At the same time I realized that it would be utterly impossible for me, a poor priest, to be so favored since the relics of identified martyrs were so rare."[13]

Don Francesco admits he was really ashamed to let anyone know how sympathetic he felt toward this young Saint. Tears filled his eyes and sentiment choked his throat. This holy priest in his heart was conscious of the deepest love he had ever felt in his life. Only God could really know of this, so he must leave the decision in the hands of the clergyman who had first suggested these priceless relics to him, and trust in God to quiet the passionate fire in his soul.

He says he retired to his room where alone with his thoughts he prayed. Despite the rashness of hoping for such a precious relic, hope gripped him with Ixion persistence. The priest had not realized that the custodian was observing him in the Treasure Room, when the uncovered relics of the Saint affected him so intensely.

Judging from that reaction, it would seem that the little martyr was destined for Don Francesco. For days he waited. The relics were not delivered. When he inquired about the delay he was informed that first-class relics bearing names are rare. The custom is to present them only to bishops for cathedrals or large congregations.[14] The explanation was given with kindness, but it wounded the heart of the gentle priest.

[13] *Ibid.*, p. 16.
[14] *Ibid.*, p. 17.

The St. Philomena relics were considered famous. They were too valuable for his hillside church. They were to be reserved for some distinguished prelate. Only three years had passed since the precious sarcophagus had been unearthed. There might be some controversy over a too hurried presentation of the girl's relics. That term of endearment sparkling on the slabs that sealed her tomb had some specific meaning.

The obscurity that had shrouded the girl for so many years might someday be unveiled. The unusual effect these relics had on the priest convinced the custodian that some special power could be exerted by this Virgin-Martyr. She must be safeguarded in the Church Treasury until a renewed search could be instituted regarding her history.

So the arguments went, and all too poignantly the terse clipped reasons re-echoed in the mind of the poor priest from Mugnano. Don Francesco did not censure the custodian for his prudence. It was in keeping with Church regulations for the Officer General to be cautious in bequeathing sacred bodies. As a good Christian, the priest bowed to the decision. If God willed him to accept another relic instead of the coveted *Filumena,* he would obey with faith. He would struggle to obey with love. Man's will athwart God's will makes a cross.[15]

Don Francesco decided to go alone to one of the canons of St. Peter's and again petition for a relic. He put his request in the name of his constant friend, the Bishop of Potenza. This canon gladly presented the relic of St. Ferma from his own private chapel to Don Francesco, since the young priest was so intent on having a girl saint for his parish in Mugnano.[16]

This prompt response was somewhat of a reproach to those who had so glibly promised and then denied him the relic of St. Philomena. Those involved in the earlier petition now decided to further their efforts, this time directly for the Bishop of Potenza. The name of Bartolomeo di Cesare was in itself worthy of a first-class relic.

15 *Ibid.,* pp. 14–20.
16 *Ibid.,* p. 21.

Soon after the arrival of St. Ferma at the lodging of Don Francesco great excitement burst at the headquarters of Don Bartolomeo. Behold, the body of St. Philomena arrived in an expensive silk-lined case! This time the young priest firmly refused their offer, saying that he would be satisfied with the relic he already had. He would keep it in his private chapel and bequeath it to his parish at Mugnano after his death.

The wisdom of the bishop prevailed. He accepted the contested relic of St. Philomena with genuine appreciation; then ordered it to be taken to the room of his secretary for safekeeping.[17] Don Francesco bowed to the voice of his bishop.

By this time several other relics had been presented to the Neapolitan priest but it was the coming of St. Philomena that attracted attention. Before long the clergy were calling at the hotel to visit Don Francesco. They were curious to see the reliquary of this Girl Saint whose popularity was mounting by the hour. The young priest claims he felt a spiritual presence that left him the moment he stepped from his room. He seemed to hear an interior voice pleading with him to accept as his own the sacred body of St. Philomena, which his cherished friend, the bishop, intended him to have.

The worry of these private admonitions caused Don Francesco deep concern and, coupled with the humid heat of the Campagna, worry took its toll. He became desperately ill. The emotional struggle overwhelmed him. On his knees he made a promise. He would bury his pride and accept from the bishop the relics of St. Philomena. These are his exact words:

"My holy Martyr, Philomena, if this matter is supernatural, if this is your plan because you wish to come with me, a miserable sinner and unworthy priest of Jesus Christ, give me a miraculous sign. Give back to me at this very moment tranquillity to my troubled soul. Let me be delivered from this struggle that has been martyring me these several days. If I obtain this grace, and rest tonight, I promise to choose you for my advocate and take you to my homeland."[18]

17 *Ibid.*, p. 22.   18 *Ibid.*, p. 23.

The earnest young priest was suddenly transformed into a different state of mind. He became cheerful, calm, and peaceful. After a night of untroubled sleep he awakened the next morning, Saturday, without a single agitating thought. Serenity had come to stay with him. His mind was all at ease.[19]

He explained the entire matter to his friend, the Bishop of Potenza, who was much relieved by the changed attitude of Don Francesco. The two men agreed that St. Ferma would be transferred to the bishop, for some church in his new diocese. The sacred remains of Philomena would be conveyed to Naples with due ceremony in the bishop's carriage, and then be presented to Don Francesco for enshrinement in Mugnano.

It was truly evident that Philomena wanted to go with the poor parish priest to help his people. The sensible bishop dismissed the traditional idea about reserving this latest treasure for a member of the hierarchy or a famous church.

Soon after the consecration of Don Bartolomeo, the homeward trip to Naples was planned for July 1, 1805, to avoid the malaria of the late summer in the Pontine marshes. The day of departure called out many friends the Neapolitans had made during their two months in Rome. Gifts and blessings were exchanged. It was a gala farewell. Everyone had been pleased with the two visitors.

Laughing and talking and milling back and forth on the Roman cobbles, the crowd seemed to be jostling the carriage. So the bishop reasoned when he felt a jolt on the back of his shins. Calling the coachman to adjust the luggage which seemed to be tumbling about, the jolly prelate stepped out of the carriage to say a fond word of departure to a few late-comers. Then a second time he seated himself for the journey, and a second time he was conscious of a rap on the back of his legs. Somewhat testily he reminded his man to wedge the luggage more securely. The rather embarrassed coachman assured his master there could be no further disturbance now that every valise had been tied in. When the bishop felt the third blow

[19] *Ibid.*, p. 24.

he was mystified. His impatience let loose. He jumped up and began to investigate, insisting that cloaks and satchels be completely rearranged.

The two clergymen were more than dismayed when the coachman dragged from under their seats the small black ebony case, that precious casket holding the sacred remains of the Virgin-Martyr. There it had been on the floor of the carriage, under all the trappings, and the two men planked on top! They were panicky within.

The poor servant hurried to explain: "Your Lordship warned me to see that the black case was firmly placed so that it would be well protected on the homeward trip. As you see, I was careful to lodge it snugly in the corner and pile everything on top. It is mysterious, Your Honor. That case has worked itself loose and upset all the baggage. Please, Your Highness, tell me, shall I pack it in again?"

This time the Bishop of Potenza managed the situation. He recalled that he had promised Philomena a place of honor. Deeply moved by the unexpected incident, the two clergymen lifted the reliquary to the seat opposite theirs. Down on their knees they went in veneration, passing out of the vicinity of St. John Lateran, leaving Rome in silent prayer.[20]

This prodigy the bishop himself publicized in Naples. He had been deeply touched by the reminder from the young Virgin-Saint. Not even a high-ranking ecclesiastic dare be unmindful of the honor due God's band of saints. Pledges made to heaven are binding. People of every rank heard the comments of the new bishop. Don Francesco mentions a few names, among them the Canon of Nola who was Don Alessandro di Gennaro. Another was the Procurator of Mugnano at that time, Don Domenico Tedeschi.[21]

Cecily Hallack quotes from Father Bowden's story of Philomena that the clergymen knelt most of the way as the carriage rolled along. They say they sat only to recite the Psalms and read aloud from spiritual books. They sang hymns and prayed as though they were making a solemn pilgrimage. Before them was the shrine, "wonders hidden in wood and wrappings"; the guard of honor, the two reverent churchmen with uncovered bowed heads.[22]

Due to the presence of the Saint, no doubt, the carriage traveled from Rome to Naples in one day, whereas the journey to the Holy City had taken three days.

It is to be noted also that special protection seemed to be evidenced on the return trip at the time the horses slipped and the carriage dipped into a ditch along the road. The riders were not at all perturbed. They just continued on chanting their prayers or lost in silent meditation. They knew of the accident only after they had covered their mileage, and were informed by the coachman how close they had all been to a fatal mishap.

It is true there are spiritual affinities that link us with angels and saints. Otherwise Don Francesco, the timid priest from a small town, says he could not have braved the idea of becoming not only the depositor but the master of a precious relic of a recent find.

[22] Hallack, p. 21.

CHAPTER III

Stopover in Naples

IN THE PRESENCE OF THE NEWLY CONSECRATED BISHOP OF POTENZA the relics were uncovered in Naples in the private chapel of the villa owned by Don Antonio Terres, a bookdealer, and his wife, Donna Angela Rose, the victim of an incurable disease that had caused the family a decade of anxious years.[23]

There is nothing stiff or unbending or blindly rigid about true piety. The wealthy family that had invited the bishop and the priest to stop over with them were quite flattered by the episcopal carriage coming up their driveway, with a saintly young lady riding in state. The bishop's "Little Queen of Hearts" was destined to receive all the deference the rich household could bestow.

The relics had been encased in a richly adorned casket, bound with bands of red silk, to which many Spanish seals had been attached by the gentlemen friends of the bishop. All present were conscious of that rare fragrance that perfumed the Terres house all the time the sacred virginal body reposed there.

The relics consisted of five parcels, each wrapped in snowy cotton, and duly sealed. One contained the vase of St. Philomena's blood. The skull and other parts of the head were wrapped separately. Three other parcels contained the bones and the ashes of the other parts of her body.[24]

Spectators at the original exhuming of the sacred remains

23 Don Francesco, p. 86.
24 Ibid., p. 87.

24

had declared that the body seemed to be intact, but the air caused its disturbance. It is understandable that after three more years, and the translation from the cemetery to the Roman Treasure House of Relics, and the carriage ride from Rome to Naples, the ashes now evident had been the flesh of the martyred girl.

The bones were small and unbroken. Only the skull had been fractured, at the base. The teeth remained.

Donna Angela offered to attire the relics with the hope of being cured of her infirmities. Actually she was completely restored to health that week.[25]

After the vesting had been authorized by the Bishop of Potenza, Donna Terres and Don Francesco spared neither time nor money in selecting Philomena's finery. Unfortunately the fashion designer who prepared the papier-mâché corpus for the encasement of the bones lacked the artistic touch. Instead of forming a genteel, dainty-looking girl of teen age, his Neapolitan tastes designed a robust mature young woman. Along some lines the image was unlovely. Certainly it was not all loveliness in the sense the good bishop and the priest had desired. They were both too courteous to openly disapprove. They just hoped and hoped, not realizing what they hoped for. But when the young Saint altered her own appearance, in a miraculous manner, the wise men understood. That is what we imply from Don Francesco's memoirs. We are not discussing the "miracle," nor at any point do we confuse the unusual with an article of faith.

The relics of the martyr's skull were rewrapped in clean cotton, then sealed and placed in the artifact head, which the artist had formed of wax over the skull. Several teeth were fitted behind the lips which were opened slightly with a knife. The one tooth showing deformed the mouth. This was in direct contrast with the closed eyes, a lack of harmony produced when the model maker molded the waxy preparation over the skull, working it down over the eye sockets like the eyelids of a person asleep. In a most unskillful way he painted the hands

[25] *Ibid.*, p. 89.

and face, the neck and shoulders an ugly whitish color. Don Francesco loudly protested, but to no avail.[26]

The bones of the other parts of the body were joined together with very fine wires. Later they were fastened with high-grade rubber. Finally muslin was considered best to make the joints flexible.

The parcels containing the ashes and small fragments of bone were deposited in the bones of the corpus. Two splinters from the True Cross of Christ were enclosed in the same hollow of the bosom, near the heart of the corpus. The seams were then triple-sealed by the Bishop of Potenza in the presence of Don Francesco and the Terres family and a notary.[27]

To have a saint for a friend is a reasonable desire. To actually clothe the body of a saint was a supreme joy that performed a miracle in Donna Angela Rose. Her illness, pronounced incurable by the most renowned physicians of Naples, left her immediately. The moment she touched the sacred relics every trace of her malady disappeared.

Assisted by her two daughters, and supervised by Don Francesco, the happy mother attired the papier-mâché image in a white underrobe and stockings. Over a fine linen skirt went a silk skirt, then an expensive dress of white silk, emblem of virginity. Philomena was a virgin. In the hierarchy of merit virginity is second only to martyrdom. Philomena was also a martyr. To symbolize martyrdom, the outer garment was deep red, designed along the lines of a Grecian style.

Over one shoulder Donna Angela draped an azure blue scarf of finer texture than the purple-red velvet robe. Over the wig of dark chestnut-colored silk thread, which hung long and straight, was placed a floral crown of gold and silver twist. In one gloved hand of the image Donna Terres placed an arrow, with the point directed to Philomena's heart. In the left hand the Saint received both a palm and a lily.

[26] *Ibid.*, p. 90.
[27] *Ibid.*, p. 91.

Pleased with her sincere artistic endeavor, Donna Terres maternally laid the "dollish" Sleeping Beauty on a couch of silk, with two grand cushions of the same material pillowed under the head. Then the good-intentioned woman eyed her handiwork with that sense of happiness that accompanies a service for a loved one. Her Philomena, her Saint, was ready now to meet her friends.

But alas! The glass-sided ebony shrine, the gift of the new Bishop of Potenza, had been measured to fit the five-foot corpus. Now with all the fluffiness in the satiny-silk lining of the mat on which the Saint was to repose, plus the puffiness of the embroidered cushions, plus the heavy robes, the arrow, the anchors, the palm and the lily, the slippers and the jeweled crown — there was not enough space for even a little Girl Saint to relax!

Don Francesco was embarrassed beyond expression with the finished job. Certainly he was not pleased with the unbecoming posture of his Virgin-Saint's slightly elevated knees. But what was Donna Terres to do? It was not her fault the clergyman had ordered the shrine just the size of the corpus. They had meant well, she knew. But she said to herself that only a woman knows how to allow enough breathing space for clothes. These well-meaning gentlemen had not approximated even one extra inch.

Obviously the modest Virgin-Saint was more than intolerant about her graceless position, as she proved soon after when she deliberately discarded one of her stuffy cushions, changed over to a somewhat side-facing attitude, and relaxed like a saint.[28]

Then came the great day for the Bishop of Potenza, the priest from Mugnano, and the Terres household. Majestically before them in their own chapel was the body of a Saint on whom they had lavished their love and their gold. Their friends flocked to view the heavenly guest. By this time the people had heard of the new Saint.

[28] *Ibid.*, p. 91.

Upon the request of Don Vincenzo di Amico, pastor of the Church of Sant' Angela in Naples, the reliquary was transferred in solemn procession through the village and exposed on the altar of St. Lucy, on the Epistle side of the church. For three days and nights the shrine was lighted by eighteen candles weighing a half pound each. During that vigil no public miracles were performed.

The priests of that church cheerfully confessed afterward to Don Francesco that they had been determined to keep the relic there if *one miracle* took place. Don Francesco knowingly smiled. His Philomena was bound for Mugnano. Naples had relics of its own. The Saint purposely reserved her miraculous powers while exposed to the congregation of Naples, it would seem.

After the relics were reinstated in the Terres chapel several acutely sick persons were cured. A lawyer, Don Angelo Antonio Montuori, testifies he was present on August 7, 1805, when his attorney friend, the famous Don Michele Ulpicella, walked out of the Terres chapel a healed man. The day before Don Michele had been carried in on a litter, an invalid suffering for the past six months with painful sciatica. His day of prayer at the Saint's shrine had been rewarded. Publicly he drew up a legal document regarding his immediate cure.[29]

Just before the triumphal journey to Mugnano on August 9, 1805, Don Francesco presented Donna Angela Rose the only key to the shrine to soothe her longing to keep the Saint close by. To be selected as key holder certainly was an honor. Only Donna Terres could unlock the shrine.

To avoid gathering a crowd that might detain them, the cortege set out by moonlight late that evening. One of the two porters, who had come from Mugnano to help transport the relics, developed an attack of nephritis. At the suggestion of Don Francesco, this porter, mentioned as Stefano Guerriero, asked the Saint to be relieved immediately so that he could help to carry the new shrine. The sciatica pain disappeared as

[29] *Ibid.*, p. 92.

he lent his shoulder to the weight. He declared he could carry the reliquary by himself. It had only "feather lightness."[30]

Don Francesco's maiden sister and several other pious pilgrims chanted the rosary as they journeyed on, respectfully concerned about disturbing the sleeping city. About midnight the sky clouded and a threatening storm gathered. Perhaps Philomena desired the spotlight of attention again. As soon as she was invoked to roll back the clouds, a space in the sky seemed to clear. Don Francesco says the moon began to shine full and bright, surrounded by stars, lighting the whole journey to Mugnano like a column of fire amid the pitch darkness of the surroundings.

Shrine bearers in the night, their prayerful hearts stirred as their tread re-echoed on the cobbled road. The heavens seemed now ready to part and send forth a trumpeter angel to announce a new saint in the galaxy of the stars.

In the vicinity of Cimitile, a hamlet in the district of Nola, the shrine suddenly seemed to be weighted with lead. When the porters rested the case on the ground they heard a metallic sound as though bronze had struck the earth. The priest was mystified. Then as from his subconscious mind he vaguely remembered.

They had halted near the public wayside cross in front of the church that formerly belonged to the religious of St. Francis of Paula.[31] This salutation of the little Virgin-Martyr was not mere ecclesiastical etiquette, such as she politely practiced in the Archdiocese of Naples, where her relics had such fervid reception. Here in the suburb, Cimitile, thousands of martyrs had suffered under the Roman emperors. Their memory merited respect.

One of the shrine bearers who had witnessed the re-echo of the ground when the weight was rested, and then assisted in raising the shrine, which again seemed to lose its weight just outside the village of Schiawa, prayed aloud: "A miracle! The

[30] *Ibid.*, p. 95.
[31] Hallack, p. 25.

Saint has become as light as a feather again, just as she was at Naples!"[32]

About six in the morning, Don Francesco had sent messengers into Mugnano for additional porters to lift the leadenlike body from the Cimitile road. These porters arrived to assist at about seven that night, August 10, 1805. They were told to join the procession because of their generosity in answering the priest's call for help, but they were no longer needed as weight bearers. The temporary and unexplainable heaviness of the shrine had disappeared as miraculously as it had come.

[32] Don Francesco, p. 97.

CHAPTER IV

Welcome to Mugnano

STILL MILES AWAY ON THE NAPLES ROAD troops of people from neighboring villages came cheering along, waving olive branches and shouting: *Viva la Santa!* ("Long live the Saint.") When they saw the shrine decked with flags and flowers they danced before it, until their explosive Neapolitan emotion burst out of control. By the time the cortege reached Mugnano, the milling crowd was so hilarious, Don Francesco found it impossible to proceed into the church destined to receive the relics.

To calm the people's fervor, Don Francesco intoned the Litanies, and while the crowd fairly shouted the responses and bowed their heads, the shrine was conveyed into the home of Don Diego di Napoli. This suing for time enabled the clergy to form an orderly procession, in keeping with the dignity of a saint.[33]

While the concourse of people was surging around the courtyard of this house, a whirlwind seemed to gather force, and the crowd grew panicky. The fury of the wind caused Don Francesco to fear its demoniacal power might strike at the couch of the Saint. But upon approaching the casket, the winds ceased.

A zealous priest took advantage of the lull to shout in a strong voice: "Christians, do not be afraid, for these are scarecrows from the princes of darkness, who well know this holy martyr, the account of her victories over them and their principality. Now this martyr is made known to the faithful as a shining star, coming forth from the darkness of the catacombs. Through her

[33] *Ibid.,* p. 109.

merit in the eyes of God, her victorious soul in heaven shall continue to give battle against these apostate and condemned spirits. She will obtain untold graces for the Christians of this district, to whom God had given her. That is why these ugly enemies of our Saint show themselves in these extraordinary signs to be afflicted, humiliated, and in despair."[34]

This reasonable admonition quieted the fear though not the storm. Still, during the two hours the procession wound around the village to the church, not a single candle was extinguished. The six tapers blazed gloriously into the heavens though the whirlicane devil-danced around and around the shrine. The old porters who had carried it all the way from Naples had the place of honor at the head. The others were at the rear. Triumphantly they moved on, the surging van of people praying aloud. Drums beat and fifes played, while the church bells across the country rang out an answer to the silvery tones that pealed from the belfry of Our Lady of Grace.

The Saint had come! Under a fine canopy the shrine was deposited near the Gospel side of the high altar. A Mass of thanksgiving was sung, and a holy day of obligation was proclaimed for the Diocese of Nola. It was early dawn, the eleventh of August, 1805.[35]

That memorable Sunday morning Don Francesco made a formal and official presentation of the relics of St. Philomena to the people of Mugnano. This he tells in his memoirs, published in 1829. The deed of donation was recorded by the notary, Don Tommaso di Andrea.[36]

For several weeks the people continued their fervent prayer, returning again and again to gaze lovingly on what they deemed the most beautiful sleeping princess from Paradise. Though she seemed not to see through her closed eyelids, she obviously heard their pleas for help.

With simple faith they talked to her, calling attention to gangrened arms, blind babies, worried wives, and stiffened old men.

[34] *Ibid.*, pp. 104–105.   [35] *Ibid.*, p. 105.   [36] *Ibid.*, pp. 107–108, 120.

On record is the sudden cure of a poor man who had been invalided for months. This bedridden victim of gout, said to be Angelo Bianco,[37] prayed to be able to get to Mugnano to see the precious relics. He vowed on that Friday night when the procession started from Naples that he would join the praying crowd if he could only walk by morning.

His prayer seemed not to pierce the heavens. The pain intensified, but old Angelo repented his past anticlericalism and renewed his act of faith. "His hope increased also." When he heard the bells and the bombs heralding the approaching procession, Angelo struggled from his couch and painfully dressed in his best. Somehow he tumbled himself out to the road. Instantly he realized his miraculous cure. He ran, waving his cane and shouting the good news.

On the octave day of the translation from Naples to Mugnano other wonders were witnessed by the crowds, who had prayed all through the novena for more miracles. While the choir sang during the solemn Mass, one mother, Angela Guerriero, bowed her head in submission to God's will. She had been so hopeful that her crippled child would walk. All the villagers sympathized with the poor widow whose little Modestino could not move his feet. For ten years she had carried her little boy from doctor to doctor. No cure seemed possible. Surely the young Girl Saint would intercede for the child. Now the last day of the novena had come and still the mother prayed.

Disturbed by a slithering noise, Angela raised her head, fearing the child had slipped to the floor. To her astonished eyes heaven seemed to open. There was her Modestino, running up the aisle. Impulsively she rushed after the child, frightened by the shock. But when the little boy knelt before the flowery shrine, dazzling bright with lights and banners, a cry of "Miracle!" burst from the congregation.

After the Mass a solemn *Te Deum* rang from the hearts of all who had seen the boy walk for the first time in ten years. Together he and his mother gave public testimony as they

[37] Hallack, p. 32.

paraded through the streets that day, acclaiming the power of their Philomena, the wonder-working Saint.[38]

Perhaps it is the appeal of youth that called forth the help of the young Saint for children in distress. Some of the stories told are like fairy tales, but true. A few of them are quite refreshing.

Among the concourse of people who flocked to Vespers at the end of that first memorable novena, honoring the Saint of Mugnano, was a mother with a child blinded by smallpox. Even the most celebrated specialists had not convinced her that her two-year-old child would never see, that sight was hopelessly impaired by disease.

From the village of Avella she had traveled, but her speed was impeded by the weight of the child. She was obliged to stand out in the sun with hundreds who reached the church after its capacity overflowed into the street. Determined that nothing would block her passage to the shrine, the distraught mother shouldered her way through the crowd, while the priest, Don Antonio Vetrano, preached on God's power channeled through the saints.

News of the crippled child's cure had grapevined through the village since noon. This mother trusted in the goodness of the Girl Saint to clear her child's vision by some miraculous intervention. With naïve directness the mother dipped her finger into the oil from the lamp burning before the shrine, and anointed the closed, scarred eyelids of her child.

What a spectacular move! Feeling the warmth of the holy oil, the baby chuckled with childish pleasure. And when she saw the light, her little hands grabbed for the lamp, and her chubby finger pointed up at the preacher and back to the gayly decked shrine. Playfully the baby gave thanks in a baby way.

Irrepressible emotion flooded the church. The people outside clamored to get in. Moved by breathless curiosity they pushed and pushed and pushed. The priest feared the outcome of

[38] *Ibid.*, p. 33.

this uncontrollable emotion. If it were not immediately quieted, someone would be trampled. He shrieked until his priestly voice calmed them. Did they want to see the baby? He then commanded respect.

Stretching down, the preacher lifted the gurgling child to the pulpit. There in his arms sat a bright-eyed tiny girl. Just a blind baby only a short time before, now preaching silently the most eloquent sermon to blind souls.[39]

The popularity of St. Philomena grew so rapidly Don Francesco saw the need of erecting a small chapel for the relics. He constructed a wooden altar over which he placed the shrine. Attached to the front of the shrine was a portable screen, easy to slide away on days of solemn exposition of the relics. The simplicity of the new chapel corresponded with the poverty of the people who gave all they had to honor their beloved Saint. The new altar was dedicated on the feast of St. Michael, 1805.[40]

Philomena's guardian, Don Francesco, and his people had a pleasing surprise just about that time. The image assumed a different position. The right arm stretched itself out, holding the arrows pointing toward her feet. (Earlier these had pointed toward the heart.) The mouth opened to reveal the teeth naturally and gracefully and the color and shape of the face changed, vastly improving the inartistic mask.[41]

The sacristan screamed that day when he moved the screen for some visitors to see the shrine. In bewilderment, the pastor hurried to the chapel. He recalled the miraculous change that had taken place in the courtyard on the way from Naples, how the gentle Virgin had delicately moved herself to a modest reclining position, more edifying than the bent-knee attitude forced upon her by the ill-fitting couch.

Turned graciously to greet the people, with her head perked up in that pretty fashion, and the red mantle held as though

[39] Don Francesco, pp. 48–49.
[40] Hallack, p. 35.
[41] Don Francesco, p. 121.

she would protect all Mugnano under it, Philomena was lovely. But it was the heavenly smile on her beautiful face that captivated the priest. She seemed such a gentle maiden, serene and rested looking.

That day the Bishop of Carinola, whose name is recorded as Don Salvatore di Lucia, had offered Mass in Philomena's chapel. Both he and Raffaele di Amico, brother of the pastor of the church where Philomena had been venerated in Naples, testified to this miraculous change in the shrine. The evidence that no earthly interference was possible is the fact that only one key was available, the key held by Donna Angela Terres in Naples.[42]

Legal procedure required a solemn deposition by Donna Terres that the key was constantly in her possession and had never left her. The artist gave under oath his testimony that he had not repainted the image. It was in its normal whiteness when he last saw it. Thousands who had viewed the shrine witnessed the change that had occurred, although the triple seals impressed by the episcopal ring were still intact.

After that countless cures were recorded, and patrons of the shrine declared they had received favors for body and soul. "Father Charles Bowden of the Oratory, in his writing on the wonders wrought by the intercession of Saint Philomena, states that wonders overflowed like the waters of a stream damned up. . . ."[43]

Today in the sanctuary of St. Philomena there are no *ex-votos*. They have become so numerous and of such great variety, they would give the place a cluttered-up appearance. They are now preserved for examination in the Tesoro or Treasury of the Saint, where the walls are literally covered with them. These offerings give silent witness to the numberless marvels of the shrine. Wax models of beautiful babies, arms, legs, and other parts of the body, in the silver silence speak the language of a grateful people. The babies represent fulfillment of a desire for

[42] *Ibid.*, pp. 129–131.   [43] Hallack, p. 39.

family life, or the assistance of the Virgin-Saint in time of childbirth.

The waxen members of the body symbolize fingers and toes, hands and feet, arms and legs that have been restored to health. Glass eyes and teeth tell of improved vision and relief from toothache. Crutches, canes, litters, and wheel chairs are evidence of disuse. The owners cast them aside after Philomena exercised her power with God. Among this collection is the reclining couch on which Pauline Marie Jaricot was carried to the shrine in Mugnano. She no longer used the invalid couch after her miraculous cure in 1835.

At one time a child's curls were left at St. Philomena's feet in gratitude for the walking power regained by the boy who had not used his legs in twelve years. His mother had taken him to the shrine in Mugnano. After several days of prayer without a visible response the disappointed parents carried the limp child out to the carriage and drove away with crushed hearts. When they reached home the child got up and walked out of the carriage into the house, unaided.

It is said that love transforms the true lover into a resemblance of the object of his passion. When Philomena smilingly gazed on her many devotees, the youth of Mugnano were chastened and exalted by the presence of their Virgin-Saint. Timid girls were gently fired by noble aspirations when they appealed to her for guidance. Carefree and fun-loving young men came to convince themselves that this maiden had braved the executioner's blade to preserve her virginity. Many a cavalier saluted this young girl who had refused the love of an emperor, so the legend tells, because not even a princess may marry a man who holds a lawfully wedded wife. This Philomena, "Princess of Paradise," who might have been consort of Rome and Greece, preferred to be fastened with an anchor around her neck and cast into the Tiber, rather than to be floated in the tide of unholy love. But there were skeptics then as there are today.

There came a cynic to Philomena's celebrated shrine. She was a woman with a narrow horizon, a nagger, no doubt, who had learned only one tune and then lost all ear for music. Philomena's popularity grated on this unbeliever, Marianna Masuccia, wife of Andrea Tedeschi.

Daringly this middle-aged woman stood before the shrine, demanding a miracle: "How is it possible that the Saint can open her eyes when she has none beneath those closed eyelids? How could such a thing happen to a face made of papier-mâché? If she shows this wonder to others, why not to me?"

The Saint opened her eyes, which were then severe, pierced them contemptuously on Marianna, and then sweetly closed them, leaving Marianna in a paroxysm of fear and contrition.[44]

The Saint had been in Mugnano a year. Preparations were under way for the first great festive day, August 11, 1806. At that time Napoleon's brother, Joseph, had his troops quartered in the vicinity. This army of occupation came in with the victory of the Napoleonic power over Ferdinand, King of Naples and Sicily, in December, 1805.

There was general consternation in the village two nights before the feast when two hundred and forty soldiers marched in. With an eye of suspicion raised to quell what seemed to him a complot to overthrow the Bonapartist government, the commanding officer steeled himself for action.

The moment had come for the Saint to assert her power. The trusting people invoked her aid, and Philomena took command. The officer, who had been marking time, suddenly realized there was nothing suspicious about this celebration which peacefully continued to get under way. His better judgment restrained his earlier convictions. And his finer sense whispered that a people who pray together will work together, because prayerful people are peaceful people, not given to political unrest.

With amazing graciousness the commander's unfriendly manner changed. He granted permission to carry on the celebration. A gala spirit filled the whole town. High officers in full dress

---

[44] Don Francesco, pp. 133–135.

and soldiers in parade attire participated. French troops divided into various detachments and contributed to the pomp of the festivity. The whole uniformed regiment saluted the little Girl Saint and formed a guard of honor all night. Bells rang and everyone who could walked to the shrine to keep a night of prayer. The so-called "enemy" had no need for vigilance. They also prayed.

On the morning of the eleventh the "horse soldiers" formed two wings to the right and left as they marched behind the statue of St. Philomena in the procession. Officers showed their respect by carrying their hats under their arms as they joined in the ceremony. Napoleon's band took turns with the drums and flutes of the village. Nothing marred the perfection of that first anniversary day. The little lady in the shrine had many admirers.

And unexpectedly the following day the high command in Naples recalled the troops. To the relief of the poor villagers the problem of feeding horses and men had been solved.

Chapels were erected by the rich throughout Italy. Statues and pictures copied from the original shrine were circulated in loving gratitude for favors received.

"In the city of Genoa, in less than eight months after her picture was exposed to public veneration in the church of the Jesuits, more than twelve hundred ex-votos in silver were offered at her shrine, besides many of gold and jewels."[45]

The people themselves were the best publicity agents. The marble cutter who had given evidence that the image had opened her eyes and smiled in a pleasing manner, and even changed the color of her face at times, is a reliable witness. This impression is recorded by many.[46]

True biography is the reconstruction of a personality, the re-discovery of a soul. It is an intimate portrait, possessing certain charm, gaiety, and understanding. Don Francesco di Lucia is

[45] Hallack, p. 42.
[46] Don Francesco, pp. 124–125.

certainly sincere in his attempt to tell the story of Philomena of Mugnano. He loves his subject. His one hope is to create in others a real devotion to the Girl Saint he went to Rome to find, the Philomena he carried back to his Neapolitan town, the lovely Maiden whose virgin body attracted more than all the wiles of the famous George Sand. Just at the time the glamour of Madame Dudevant was breaking the morale of musicians, the chaste restraint of Philomena was winning the hearts of scholars, nobility, churchmen, and the man in the crowd.

Don Francesco longed to have the world know about the gentle girl who miraculously affixed a handle to the top of a mold, thus relieving the foundrymen who feared they had miscalculated when casting a bell. He could cite instances when beautiful babies were born to mothers, though doctors feared sterility; and he could recount the time when the Terres mansion was protected by a sudden light at night, just at the moment burglars were about to break in and rob the family.

This and much more Don Francesco assembled in the account he wrote from his firsthand personal knowledge of Philomena. He had pigeonholed everything in his photographic mind. The first narrative sold out so completely, he re-edited the story soon after, and by 1829 realized the need for a third edition.

But the incident that follows refers to that very first book, called *The Story of the Miracles of St. Philomena,* published in 1826. It seems that Don Francesco ordered an extra allotment from Naples when he sensed that his supply of books was near exhaustion. The publisher's remainder numbered 221, all of which he sent to the author upon rush-order request.

To protect the books from the roadside dust, Don Francesco covered four of the five stacks on his library table, leaving one pile available for ready use. After distributing the books for a few months, he suddenly awakened to the fact that the original uncovered stack of 45 books then contained many more and the other four piles were still untouched. His unbelieving eyes saw, one evening as he entered his supply room, many copies of the book lying on the floor and strewn across the chairs. Yet the four stacks on the table were still intact.[47] Actual counting of the books on the floor and chairs totaled 72. Undoubtedly Philomena intended to prove her pleasure regarding his story. She was not the kind of saint who wished to "go out of print." She had been isolated from her fellow men for more than a century and a half. This book of Don Francesco's was meant to be a pipe line of information to all who would read. She herself would be the press agent. Those who really know and love St. Philomena appreciate her high-powered salesmanship.

[47] *Ibid.,* p. 228.

CHAPTER V

Changes With Time

IN MANY CHAPELS, reddened by the setting sun, the saints rest silently, waiting for someone to love them, we are told. The little Saint of Mugnano had many to love her, but not an edifice worthy of her greatness.

The southern half of Italy, under the Napoleonic scepter from 1806 to 1815, had felt the aftermath of frustration. In their train the French brought irreligion and unbelief. There were quarrels, sedition, and bloodshed everywhere. The peaceable peasants trembled in their homes, or fled to the mountains to avoid the hard rule of the despots. For this reason the daily gathering at the shrine of St. Philomena was sometimes interfered with. Though it dwindled, it never ceased altogether. The poor were unable to build the grand chapel they had intended for the Saint, but the upper classes continued to frequent the shrine.

Among these one day came a rich barrister from Naples, a distinguished attorney named Don Alessandro Serio. He and his wife, Donna Giovanna Fusco, had an estate in Mugnano, but it was more than material interest that prompted their visit in 1814. The truth is they came to seek a cure. The best medical skill had failed to relieve the internal malady that sapped the energy of Alessandro, who was also spiritually infirm.

During the octave of the novena in honor of St. Philomena public prayers were offered but no response came. On the eighth day of the novena the sick man's condition became so acute he had to be removed to his hotel.

When he sank into unconsciousness, his good wife desperately seized the picture of St. Philomena from the wall, and

pleaded that her dying husband be granted the grace to make
a sincere confession. By that time she had resigned herself to
God's will in refusing to cure the invalid.[48]

"Taking the picture, she put it on her husband's body, vowing
that if he had the grace to receive the Sacraments, he would
put up a marble altar in the chapel of Saint Philomena. . . ."
Scarcely had the prayer been offered when Alessandro regained
consciousness and received the Sacrament of Penance. His
chronic illness disappeared. He was able to get up from his
bed and go to Mass the next morning. After receiving Holy
Communion he promised to fulfill the vow made by his wife.[49]

Together the grateful couple ordered the grandest marble
procurable. They engaged the most skilled workmen in Naples,
and contracted for a marble hall that the most fastidious of
virgin-saints would delight to call hers.

A marble cutter from Naples, Don Giovanni Cimafonte, took
the job and, while hollowing out a place for the sacred stone
in the altar of the shrine, detected a flaw. It was a long jagged
crack which tended to break the beautiful single block of marble.

Don Giovanni wept, not only because of the loss of the altar
but also because of the loss of his reputation. When he attempted to repair the saw-toothed break, the crack lengthened,
and soon only about one fourth of the original slab remained
whole.

He prayed to St. Philomena for direction. Then he supported
the slab with an iron brace underneath, and fastened the marble
for about a finger space. But the surface was not smooth. He
decided to fill in the crevice with a chalk preparation, but it left
a disturbing dark line. While he pondered what to do next, the
marble block became so solid and well blended that the darkish
line looked like a natural vein in the marble. The "finger of the
saint," aiding the hand of the workman, by a miracle joined
in its former state the marble that had been separated.

[48] Hallack, p. 47.
[49] *The Life and Miracles of Saint Philomena, Virgin and Martyr,* English
version translated from the French abridgment of the Italian of Don Francesco
di Lucia (New York: O'Shea & Co., 1865), p. 52.

A number of persons who had seen the workman using his chisel to fit the marble into place and had heard the split sympathized with the humbled man. Now they rejoiced with him. These people and the stone mason himself, Don Giovanni Cimafonte, have verified the facts.[50]

The sanctuary for years to come would present to the visitors a consoling sight for their devotion. Their attention is always attracted to the great marble slab that covers the altar, and on which are still visible the marks of a miracle.

The Archbishop of Naples presented the shrine with a large wooden image of St. Philomena. This statue was made for processional use in the first year of the Saint's arrival. The bishop suspended around the neck of the statue a reliquary containing small splinters of bone and ashes of the martyr's body. This custom of keeping some fragments separate is generally true when a saint's body is encased in an artificial covering.

In 1823, on the anniversary of the translation of Philomena's remains to Mugnano, the customary procession got under way. Gradually the bearers complained of the heaviness of the statue, a fact not evident in the eighteen previous years. Stronger men came to assist. Even with their help the men had difficulty in supporting the statue.

Simultaneously the people noticed the rosy tint that seemed to creep over the face. And the next morning visitors commented on the dewy appearance of the chin. A moisture seemed to sparkle in the August sunlight.

Don Francesco had the statue lifted down from its place above the altar, and set a guard around it to prevent the people from touching it. Upon close examination the liquid was found to be a kind of "crystalline manna." That part of the broad red ribbon which held the relic around the Saint's neck was also soaked with it.[51]

This wonder was given the character of a public miracle by the people of Mugnano. Such was its significance that by

[50] *Ibid.*, p. 53.
[51] Don Francesco, pp. 162–164.

August 22 two impressive documents had been drawn up, one signed by the pastor and priests of the district, and the other by public officials, attesting to the facts.[52]

Silk and satin, velvet and velours can lose their luster and look shoddy even on a saint after twenty terrific summers under the Italian sun. The women of Naples desired only the loveliest for their lovely Philomena, so together they pooled their artistic sense and their pennies as well. Philomena's new attire was ready for a day of reclothing, July 5, 1824.

"After Mass the glass-sided ebony case was opened ceremoniously. The body of the Saint was carried in the arms of the priest, Don Francesco, over to a table in front of the altar. There he rested the image for the solemn clothing. There were as many women attendants as there were articles of apparel. One piece at a time was held by a woman who passed it to the prelate. Together the women and the attending priest replaced an old garment with a new one. This process lasted fully five hours.

"Then the newly clothed body was carried to the new case, wherein the Bishop of Nola and his vicar placed her in approximately the same position Philomena had miraculously taken nineteen years before. The clergymen then devoutly kissed her hand. The Bishop officially sealed the new casket."[53]

Some years later, on account of the deterioration of certain parts of the figure containing the fractured skull and the rest of the Saint's body, the reliquary was again officially opened. The project was turned over to an ecclesiastical commission established for that purpose. The most necessary repairs were made, and the relics were reclothed in richer and more precious materials. There was, however, no change in the color scheme.

To safeguard the relics while these repairs were progressing, the Nola bishop imposed the penalty of excommunication on anyone who would so much as touch the least particle of them.

[52] Copies of these papers are included in Chapter XII, pages 128–130.
[53] Don Francesco, p. 186.

Upon the completion of this third clothing, a new reliquary was made, and the body was placed therein by the members of the commission. The keys were sent to the Bishop of Nola, and kept in custody by his secretary, Canon Garafalo, awaiting the date for sealing the casket.

In the meantime the bishop died, and, to avoid further delay, the metropolitan of the district, the Cardinal Archbishop of Naples, came to Mugnano for the official sealing of St. Philomena's new casket. He arrived on Saturday, September 27, 1828. The following day he celebrated Mass in St. Philomena's chapel with due ceremony and splendor. In the presence of the huge populace, he put the four seals on the reliquary containing St. Philomena's body.

The cardinal renewed also the seals on the reliquary holding the glass vase that contains the martyr's blood.[54] Ceremoniously he proceeded to the life-size wooden statue of Philomena, the one used for processions. He sealed the reliquary that hangs around the neck of that statue because it contains the bone fragments that are distributed to the hierarchy when special request is made.

When Philomena's guardian enshrined her body on August 11, 1805, he was motivated by a single-mindedness of purpose, which was the salvation of his people. His intention centered only on the spiritual. He could not foresee that the young Virgin-Martyr would popularize Mugnano with a world-wide sweep.

Philomena's sanctuary holds the secret of the permanence of eternity. Its appeal is immortalized by the wonders of the great Saint whose relics repose there. Peasant and patrician go there with their troubles and talk to her. That is what St. Philomena likes, a simplicity that lays at her feet a problem to be solved. Those who talk things over with her will find a solution.

The Saint herself has added glory to glory by evoking the appreciation of those she has helped. Tokens of their love are

[54] *Ibid.*, p. 187.

evident in the grandeur there assembled. One hundred and fifty years ago Mugnano had only a hillside chapel. Today the majestic elegance there is dignified by the expressive name, *sanctuary*. Its magnificence in money value is incalculable.

The entrance to the sanctuary is under a solid marble portal. The artistic chapel is constructed of marble from floor to ceiling. Pillars and columns are of *giallo antico*, a valuable ornamental marble found among Italian ruins. This ancient, yellowish marble is supposed to have come originally from Algeria. The noble Corinthian capitals and the altar are pure white marble, the best to be found.

To insure protection from the elements, as well as to guard the relics of the Saint, due precaution has been taken. The precious ebony shrine is built into the marble wall over the altar in St. Philomena's chapel. The front for a width of more than six feet is shatterproof plate glass.

The waxen image of the Saint reclines in a most graceful manner in the position St. Philomena herself has acquired. Resting on her silken cushions, with silver and gold twist circling her head, gold rings in her ears, and jewels on her hands, Philomena is a dazzling sight. Richly robed always, she now has an embroidered jewel trim on her gown in more recent tribute.

Philomena's costuming as well as her appearance have undergone changes just when the Saint so desired, it seems. The first unusual change was recorded in writing by Don Francesco in September, 1805, on the feast of St. Michael, when pilgrims came to visit the original shrine.

Another inexplicable change occurred in 1824 when the image seemed to lengthen. Guardians who succeeded Don Francesco have witnessed the most marvelous happenings. In 1841, while tourists knelt reverently admiring the Saint in profile, she seemed to turn completely around and face them smilingly. The pilgrims were both pleased and amazed.

On May 27, 1892, hundreds observed the image assume another position while they looked at her. Ecclesiastical authorities have approved that statement made by the entire pilgrimage.

Father Paul O'Sullivan of Lisbon declares he saw changes occur in the image during his nine days' stay in Mugnano. He still talks of the wonders experienced when he visited the shrine in 1909. He noted the color of the face change from pale to a light blush, and again to a darker red. The lips sometimes were compressed, sometimes opened. Father is keen to remark that no person or mechanism could interfere, because the shrine is encased in the marble of the wall, and is sealed and locked in three places. Key holders are in three separate towns. The Bishop of Nola is one such honored keeper of a key.

Nine silver lamps burn constantly in the sanctuary. The blood of the Saint is preserved in a clear vase, visible through one side of the rich reliquary. This relic holder and the tabernacle where it reposes are the gifts of Maria Teresa of Austria, Queen of Naples. She and her husband, Ferdinand IV of Naples, visited the shrine many times. Opposite the shrine the three terra-cotta slabs rest in a velvet case. Visitors marvel at the vividness of the lettering still readable through its glass enclosure.

CHAPTER VI

The Most Illustrious Miracle

THE SOCIETY FOR THE PROPAGATION OF THE FAITH owes its existence to Pauline Marie Jaricot, a French girl from an aristocratic family in Lyons. Pauline Jaricot's life stream flowed on, thanks to the miraculous help of St. Philomena in 1835. How Pauline and Philomena became acquainted is worthy of note.

The home of Antoine Jaricot in the south of France offered roadside courtesy to those seeking help. It is not surprising that Père de Magallon of the Brothers of St. John of God should stop there as he journeyed through Brittany taking a house to house collection of alms. His religious community of Hospital Brothers cared for incurables, the insane, and the epileptic. In appreciation for the Jaricot hospitality Père de Magallon gave the family a splinter of bone from the sacred body of Philomena.[55]

Pauline graciously accepted the relic. She had heard the Abbé Vianney, then assistant priest at Belley, speak of Philomena, the Virgin-Martyr. Devotion to this Saint had become popular in Italy. During the twenty years following the discovery of her body in 1802, Philomena had convinced the Italians of her miracle-working power. France at that time knew very little about the young Saint.

Abbé Vianney begged Pauline to get him a relic from the Brothers of St. John of God, the first to introduce Philomena to France. That was 1819, sixteen years before Philomena's canonization, but a saint recognizes a saint. Even though John

---

[55] Burton, p. 100.

Vianney was just a poor unlearned priest, his power of discernment made him aware of Philomena's greatness.

By 1835, Pauline Jaricot had encouraged many to spread devotion to Philomena, who had won the hearts of the French who knew her. Pauline attributed her missionary success to the little miracle worker. Only one shadow darkened the Jaricot's otherwise bright home. Pauline's health was waning fast.

On a day when Pauline was acutely ill after a heart attack Père de Magallon again called to visit. He encouraged Pauline to promise a pilgrimage to the shrine in Mugnano. "Go to Philomena," he urged. "She will help you."[56]

The doctor at first refused to listen to Pauline's proposal of a trip to Italy. Then he reconsidered. To please the patient he permitted her to try the journey, while assuring her family Pauline would decide to return before she traveled very far. His sanction was more like the granting of a last request to a dying person.

Accompanied by two nurses and her chaplain, Pauline painfully but bravely started on her way. Deathly pale and much exhausted, she arrived at Paray-le-Monial where she stopped to rest. After a day of prayer in the chapel of the Visitation Convent where our Lord had revealed His Sacred Heart to St. Margaret Mary, the travelers took the road again.

The strong-willed Pauline determined to stop at Rome to receive the personal blessing of the Holy Father. Traveling southeast she was delayed by another coronary flare-up. Her attendants feared for her life, but Pauline ordered her carriage to proceed on the long journey Romeward.

When the travelers neared the steep Mont Cenis Pass, Claude, the family coachman, realized the difficulty ahead. He feared frail Pauline could not endure the slow pulling of the oxen over the deeply piled snow. He talked over the problem with the chaplain, Abbé Rousselon, and the devoted attendant, Marie Melquiond. Together they tried to persuade their beloved mistress to return home to Lyons. They thought she had already

[56] *Ibid.*, p. 108.

exhausted her waning strength. She refused to retrace her steps.

Instead Pauline was thrilled by the snowy-capped peaks of the Alps. Up, up, the pilgrims climbed between earth and the high heaven. When they reached the summit Pauline's heart gladdened with the realization of God's goodness to her. She felt assured now that Providence would take her on from there. The downward trip would be less hazardous.

By special privilege the pilgrims spent that night in the Santa Casa, at the shrine of Our Lady of Loreto in Italy. The fact that she had conquered the mighty Alps in her weakened condition acted like a tonic to Pauline. She ordered the caravan on its way, suggesting night travel to avoid the intense heat of late April. But that raised the question of brigands and accidents under cover of darkness. Shocked by the timidity of her companions, Pauline reminded them to trust in the protection of our Blessed Mother and St. Philomena. After all, they had pinned blessed medals on the carriage.

At daybreak the chaplain offered the holy Sacrifice of the Mass. With the exception of responding to the rosary which they said aloud, Pauline kept silent in order to conserve her energy.

They arrived in Rome after several weeks on the way from Lyons. Road-weary, they gladly accepted shelter at the convent of Trinità dei Monti. The superior, Mère Barat, and the other nuns of the Sacred Heart welcomed their guests with that dignified warm friendliness characteristic of French nuns. Pauline, on the verge of collapse, appreciated this atmosphere of holy quiet. While she breathed in the pure, clean air of the convent gardens, the nuns prepared for her tempting trays of wholesome food, but reaction from overexertion had intensified the struggle for breath.

For the first time Pauline felt frustrated when she admitted her inability to carry on. She confided to Cardinal Luigi Lambruschini, later papal secretary of state (1836), asking him to cancel the audience he had so graciously arranged for her at the Vatican. At this point of defeat Pauline's house of dreams came tumbling about her. Her spirit had been broken — almost!

The Catholic Church is never outdone in generosity. It owed a double debt to this Jaricot girl. She had established the Society for the Propagation of the Faith and the Association of the Living Rosary. If she would force herself to come in this dying state all the way from Lyons to Rome to have an audience with the Pope, that she would have. If Pauline could not continue her journey to the Pope, then, of course, the Pope would go to her.

He came. Mère Barat and Cardinal Lambruschini remained during the interview while Gregory XVI talked with Pauline Jaricot, whom he came to visit and thank for her generous spirit of self-sacrifice.

The kind Pontiff smiled on this girl who seemed too weak to rise from her reclining couch. She discussed with the Vicar of Christ her hope of consolidating the Society of the Living Rosary by centralizing it and the Propagation of Faith Society in Rome. The Pope was amazed at the progress of her work, even then world wide. He wondered how this frail child had endured the effort.

Leaning over, he whispered a prayer that she would remember his intention when she reached heaven, for he believed the day was close. Instead, Pauline asked the Pope to pray for her to travel on to Mugnano to the shrine of Philomena, the Virgin-Martyr.

These are Pauline's time-honored words to Gregory XVI: "If on my return from Mugnano I were to come to the Vatican on foot, then would Your Holiness deign to proceed without delay to the final inquiry into the cause of Philomena?"

"That I can agree to without giving it a thought," replied the Pope, "for that would be a miracle of the first order." Then he turned to Mère Barat and said in Italian, "How ill she is! It seems to me as if she had come forth from the grave. We shall never see her again. She will never return."

The Supreme Pontiff blessed Pauline, then commended her to Cardinal Lambruschini with the admonition, "I recommend our very dear daughter to you. Grant her all there is to be granted in the way of privileges and indulgences."[57] To all appearances Pauline Jaricot was dying.

For about a month Pauline lingered on. Then she suddenly regained enough strength to take the road again. Night travel meant jolting over bumpy roads. This was just enough to aggravate the patient's heart.

Her condition became alarming. Before they reached Naples she was speechless, but she serenely pointed her finger ahead. To humor her, the coachman drove slowly on to Mugnano.

The pilgrims arrived August 8 while the bells were ringing for Vespers. When the people of Mugnano saw her they were terrified by her deathlike appearance. They carried her into the church on her reclining chair. Then they knelt at the shrine of St. Philomena and demanded a cure for the girl who had undertaken such a heroic pilgrimage.

Pauline, easily exhausted by the kindest of fine-mannered visitors at Lyons, hardly able to draw her breath, was surrounded now by an enthusiastic crowd of self-appointed attendants, who deafened her with their pleas. Like excited children the Neapolitans prayed aloud, reminding the Saint of her great power with God, telling her she must use it if she wished to keep her pretty shrine.

"Do you hear us, Philomena? If you do not cure this pious lady we will pray to you no more! We will have nothing more to do with you! Please ask God to give you power to restore her to health right now. Yes, we shall keep our word!"

Vociferously in their enthusiasm for a miracle they shouted their prayers to heaven. St. Philomena seemed to be deaf. The people had to be told that the French lady begged them to pray in lower tones or she would faint. Nothing happened that day, nor the day after. Even Don Francesco was a bit disheartened.

It was not necessary to tell them Pauline Jaricot's background. The Neapolitans had seen to it that all the village should come to pray for the generous lady who honored their Saint by coming a long distance on an invalid chair because she had faith. Surely she would be cured entirely.

On August 10, during Benediction, Pauline attempted to kneel at the shrine. Then she experienced a strange sensation. She collapsed, and Marie feared her patient had died. The attendants tried to carry away the chair. The excited Neapolitans cried out in protest. Their St. Philomena would not disappoint them. Surely not!

Pauline was not dead. By a supreme effort she managed to sign to them that she wished to be left where she was so that her last sight of the world might be the shrine which she had come so far to honor.

Her eyes were veiled as if in death. Then tears began to creep under the lids, a tinge of color came into her cheeks, her icy hands and feet felt a new warmth stealing through them, and a heavenly joy filled her soul. It was an anguished hour for those who knelt nearest the sick girl. She was perfectly still. They feared to disturb the unusual peaceful look on her face. Something had happened. *Pauline Jaricot had been cured!*

Nevertheless, she was so worn out that she dared not make the slightest sign which would have told the watching Neapolitans that their prayers had been heard, for fear of the clamor of triumph that would result. She was carried out of the church, and the next day, carried into it, as though nothing had happened, for she still felt very weak — mostly, perhaps, with emotional reaction. But that evening after Benediction, she felt stronger, and decided that when the congregation departed, she would attempt to walk to the door of the church.

She walked to the door, out of it, as far as the house where she was staying, and, what was more, up the steep staircase to her room without feeling the smallest inconvenience. *There was no longer any doubt about the miracle.*[58]

Don Francesco had witnessed many wonders performed at the shrine in the thirty years he had his treasured Virgin-Saint. This latest marvel seemed to be calling forth a warmth of feel-

[58] Hallack, p. 98.

ing, a spontaneity more explosive than a time bomb. He knew his people. They would insist on a demonstration. To please them, he followed Pauline to the hospital and urged her to walk up and down the portico, to kneel, to wave at the joyous throngs who hailed her as another saint. Pauline obeyed with the simplicity of a child. The gladness of her heart was in melody with the bells.

For days the whole-souled tones of *"Viva Santa Filomena"* sang gloriously to heaven. Pauline made her novena of thanksgiving, going first to the feet of the Saint who had cured her, then circling the town. Escorted by military guard, she led the procession and kept pace with the beat of all the drums and fifes that Mugnano could play.

In the chapel of her benefactress Pauline left the invalid chair as an *ex-voto*. It is one of many evidences of miracles at St. Philomena's shrine. Not only did Pauline consecrate herself to lifetime devotion to the Saint; she put on the habit of the Little Sisters of St. Philomena, but without the veil. Her mode of life in France at that time did not permit a veil.

On her departure from Mugnano Pauline took with her the relic presented by Don Francesco. With a grateful heart she had lavishly invested in a life-size image of St. Philomena in which the guardian of the shrine had encased the special treasure. It was a rather large splinter of the sacred bony frame of the martyred Saint. To be sure that she could spread devotion to her new patroness, Pauline carried away medals and prints and small images that had touched the vase of blood. These and the large statue left Mugnano lying on the same stretcher that had rested the body of the invalided Pauline when she entered the town just a short time before. It will be remembered that both litter and reclining chair were needed on the pilgrimage to the shrine.

Pauline was most eager to return to France where she planned to build a shrine for Philomena. This she discussed with her fellow travelers as she sat with her back to the horses, allowing the honored place for the statue in front of her. Ordinarily the supersensitive Pauline would have sickened in the intense August heat. But that ennui had now passed. Pauline was better than ever before.

The ovation that greeted the cavalcade at every inn was breath-taking, but the lovely French woman was equal to the occasion. She graciously submitted to the congratulations of friends and all the high emotion effected by her healthy happy countenance. Generously she passed out to the reaching hands the souvenirs from the shrine.

The people of Naples went all out to extend courtesy to these French pilgrims, and arranged their time so that Pauline and her escorts could get to daily Mass and receive Holy Communion.

The Bishop of Naples had come out to greet Pauline and bless her with the relic of St. Januarius, patron of that city. The papal nuncio, Monsignor Ferretti, greeted her as "Child of the City of Martyrs." He prepared her for greater activity plus the crosses that accompany success. Momentarily the brave young woman was frightened by his prophetic words: "God has made use of you and He will again make use of you. You must fortify yourself with great courage to meet His demands." Pauline remembered that warning in later years. But to God she entrusted everything.

There was secret satisfaction in learning that news of her miraculous cure had not yet been relayed to Rome. Pauline eagerly looked forward to surprising the Pope by walking in unannounced (if this could be possible). But first she must surprise the nuns at Trinità dei Monti. It was there she had stopped on the way into Rome, at the time the Holy Father had come to administer the last blessing. It was there in the presence of Mère Barat, Gregory XVI had made that memorable promise to canonize Philomena if this sick girl, Pauline Jaricot, could walk back from the shrine.

The superior at the convent urged Pauline to ask for an audience at the Vatican by appealing through the proper channels immediately. The Papal Guard admitted her incognito on the advice of Cardinal Lambruschini, and Pauline walked into the audience chamber of the Vatican, knelt before the Pope, and then rose at his suggestion before he recognized her.

Gregory XVI was startled. "Is this really my dear daughter? And has she come back from the grave, or has God manifested in her favor the power of the Virgin-Martyr?" he asked.

"It is indeed I, Your Holiness," she said. "It is the woman you saw at death's door so short a time ago. God has had compassion on me, thanks to Philomena's prayers. And I want your permission to carry out the vow I made at her shrine, to build a chapel to her in Lyons."

"Assuredly," said the Pope. "And we shall now carry out the other promise I made to you, to approve the study of her cause. And now I want you to tell me the entire story of your cure."

When she had finished, he said, "Now walk up and down before me that I may be fully convinced that this is no apparition from another world, but actually my daughter from Fourviere." He led her through several of the great rooms, urging her to walk rapidly and watching her steps intently.

As she walked back and forth in front of him, the master of ceremonies suddenly stepped up to remind her that etiquette forbade turning one's back on the Pope, and that she had done it several times.

Gregory caught the low words. "It is my fault," he said. "God has already made other exceptions in her favor — and much greater ones."[59]

Before Pauline left the audience chamber the Pope promised once again to authorize immediately and officially the examination of Philomena's cause.

Pauline agreed to remain in Rome a year so that her cure might be thoroughly investigated. During that time her strength increased. She had further communications with the Sovereign Pontiff, long talks with Cardinal Lambruschini and also Father Cipolletti, master general of the Dominicans, from whom she wished to ask an act of affiliation with all the Dominican orders for the Confraternity.

[59] Burton, p. 116.

After her return to France, Pauline built on her property a marble chapel that was a miniature reproduction of the church of Mugnano. This she dedicated to St. Philomena, promising to devote her life to the service of the poor, in honor of the beloved Virgin-Martyr.

The many *ex-votos* that eventually covered the walls of this French shrine testified that Philomena was quite active. Pilgrims came to Lyons every day. But this was only the beginning of Philomena's fame in France. The chapel built by the Curé of Ars tells more of that story.

Devotion to St. Philomena received the solemn approbation of the Church but not until frequent and fervent supplications to that effect had been sent to Rome. These many petitions came from both the people and the clergy. In the foreground were bishops appealing the cause for Philomena's canonization. Father Bowden of the London Oratory notes that the entire episcopate of Italy declared the girl, Philomena, to be a saint.

The ruling Pontiff, Gregory XVI, requested the Sacred Congregation of Rites to debate whether or not a Decree should be promulgated authorizing the public cultus of St. Philomena. Their reply was affirmative.

"The Decree, authorizing the devotion, and granting to the clergy of Nola (the diocese in which Mugnano is situated) the privilege of celebrating Mass in her honor, was published by Gregory XVI on *January 30, 1837*. In March, 1839, the same Pontiff, by Decree of the Sacred Congregation of Rites, raised her feast to a double of the Second Class.

"It is to be noted here that this is the only instance of a Proper Office being granted to a Saint from the Catacombs of whom nothing was known except her name and the bare fact of her martyrdom."[60]

[60] Father Goodman, M.S.C., *Saint Philomena, Virgin, Martyr, and Wonder-Worker* (Sydney, Australia: Pellegrini, 1931), p. 35.

CHAPTER VII

An Old Saint and a Young One

WHEN WE SAY "THE CURÉ OF ARS" we automatically think "St. Philomena." The saintly priest whose direction was characterized by common sense, remarkable insight, and supernatural knowledge credited his power to the only woman in his life, his "dear little Saint," the Virgin-Martyr, Philomena. To his memory and that of Philomena, a basilica now stands, marking the spot where his humble village church sheltered the confessional which drew to him vast crowds from far and near. His instructions were simple in language, full of imagery drawn from daily life and country scenes.

When the Curé heard the news that Gregory XVI had canonized Philomena, this holy priest lost no time in dedicating a chapel to his chosen patroness. There he exposed a relic of Philomena, a splinter of her bone. This relic Pauline Jaricot had sent him when she returned from visiting Philomena's shrine in Mugnano in 1835.

The miracles recorded by his biographers are much the same as those attributed to St. Philomena, with whom he ever seemed to walk hand in hand. These wonders generally cover the obtaining of money for worthy causes, the healing of the sick, especially children, and the acquiring of knowledge. Like Philomena, the Curé softens the hardened heart.

In writing a sketch of the Curé of Ars, Bruce Marshall says: ". . . He could not bring himself to believe that miracles could be operated through his intercession, and he was unwilling that others should attribute them to a merit which he was certain he didn't possess. He himself ascribed them to the intercession of St. Philomena . . . who, he was sure, had been responsible for his own recovery from double pneumonia in 1843. 'Go and pray before St. Philomena's altar,' he told the sick, to make sure that their recovery would be ascribed to what he honestly considered the proper source.

"A woman, who had suffered from tubercular laryngitis for eight years, came to Ars: because of her illness she couldn't speak and had to use signs or write on a slate instead. It was by the latter means that she informed the Curé of her illness. 'Go and lay your slate on St. Philomena's altar,' the Abbé Vianney told her. She did so and was cured. A mother carried her paralyzed son of eight into the sacristy for M. Vianney to bless. 'That boy's too heavy to carry,' the Curé said. 'Put him down and go and pray to St. Philomena.' Clutching his mother's hand, the boy staggered to the saint's altar and knelt there. Three quarters of an hour later he was completely cured."[61]

From the time the chapel in Ars was opened, St. Philomena seemed to draw blessings on the village. The Curé became famous as the "priest of the confessional." It was not unusual for him to spend as many as fifteen hours out of the twenty-four listening to those who knelt at his feet. Always he counted on Philomena for the answers.

Young people in doubt as to their vocation sought his advice. Bishops, priests, and nuns came to him for direction. Persons in all sorts of difficulties, the sick, the sin-burdened, confided in the holy Curé. In 1855, the number of pilgrims coming to Ars had reached twenty thousand a year. They came to visit both the saintly old priest and the young Saint.

In his own spiritual needs he counted on her help. He credited St. Philomena with extinguishing a fire in his rectory since the demonish flames stopped when they reached her picture just over his bed. On another occasion when devils seemed to buzz around him, Philomena chased them away, he believed, because he pleaded with childlike trust in her.

[61] From "The Curé of Ars" by Bruce Marshall from *Saints for Now,* copyright 1952, Sheed and Ward, Inc., New York, p. 288.

Between the Curé and Philomena there was understanding and sympathy. He credited to her all the graces and wonders of the pilgrimages to Ars. "It was all her work," he continued to say. He trusted her to intercede for him. She granted all his requests. He returned to her generous service. He was her knight; she was his lady. Theirs was a chivalrous love, according to his biographer, the Abbé Alfred Monnin.

When in May, 1843, the Curé of Ars was acutely ill, St. Philomena was invoked to save him. His cure was considered miraculous.

Mademoiselle des Garets, one of his parishioners, had written: "Our holy Curé is so ill as to make us think his crown is ready, and heaven open to receive him. He has been in bed for the last three days. The peace of heaven seems depicted on his countenance. He told me he was going to begin his preparation for death. . . . You cannot form an idea of the touching and religious spectacle continually before us since the illness of this holy man. . . . He had read the chapter of Ecclesiastes upon obedience to physicians. . . . He always shows the most perfect docility to the prescriptions of his medical attendants."

And the Abbé Renard: "An express came to me at midnight with the information that M. Vianney wished to see me. On my arrival at Ars I had the happiness of embracing the holy priest whom I found in such state of exhaustion, that his death seemed close at hand. . . ."

The Abbé Valentin, his confessor, judged it was time to administer the Last Sacraments. When the Curé was asked in the formula of the ritual whether he believed in the truths of our holy religion, he replied: "I have never doubted them"; whether he pardoned his enemies, "I have never, thank God, wished ill to anyone." In the morning the curé of Fareins said Mass for the sick priest at the altar of St. Philomena. At that very hour the patient fell, for the first time, into a peaceful slumber, which was the precursor of his perfect recovery. It was a general report at Ars that St. Philomena had then appeared to him and revealed things which, to the end of his long life, were a subject of great joy and consolation to him.

The following is the testimony of Monsieur Pertinant, the schoolmaster of Ars, who had been the affectionate and assiduous nurse of the Curé throughout his illness:

"Our holy Curé, finding himself at the last extremity, begged that a Mass might be said in honor of St. Philomena, to whom he had consecrated himself by a special vow. The Mass was said by a neighbouring priest, and all in Ars, whether residents or strangers, assisted at it. Before the holy sacrifice began, M. le Curé seemed to me to be laboring under a kind of terror. I observed something extraordinary about him — a great anxiety, an unwonted disturbance. I watched his movements with re-doubled attention, believing that the fatal hour was come, and that he was about to breathe his last. But as soon as the priest was at the altar, he became suddenly more tranquil; he looked like a man who was gazing at something pleasing and consoling. The Mass was hardly over, when he said: 'My friend, a great change has taken place in me; I am cured.' Great was my joy at these words. I was convinced that M. Vianney had seen a vision, for I had several times heard him murmur the name of his sweet patroness, which led me to believe that Saint Philomena had appeared to him; but I dared not question him."

A letter dated May 17, 1843, tells of his continued convalescence: "The strength of our holy Curé increases with a speed which his physicians call marvelous. 'Say *miraculous,*' he replied. He attributes his cure to the intercession of Saint Philomena. On May 19th, M. Vianney was so far recovered . . . he went to pay his tribute of gratitude to his miracle-working Philomena, his 'dear little Saint.' As though he had not drifted to the gates of death and back again, the holy priest resumed his strenuous duties until his holy death in 1859."

While Archbishop of Westminster, Dr. Manning, later Henry Cardinal Manning, spoke of the bond of devotion the celebrated Curé of Ars had with his "dear little Saint": "Mysterious and wonderful is the sympathy which thrills through the com-munion of saints, unbroken by distance, undimmed by time, unchilled by death! The youthful saint went forth from her mother's arms to die for Christ; the lictor's ax cropped the budding lily, and pious hands gathered it up and laid it in the tomb; and so fifteen centuries went by, and none on earth thought upon the virgin martyr who was following the Lamb withersoever He went, till the time came when the Lord would have her glory to appear; and then He chose a champion for her in the lonely toil worn priest to whom he had given a heart as childlike, and a love as heroic as her own; he gave her to be the helpmate of his labors, and bade her stand by him to shelter his humility behind the brightness of her glory lest he should be affrighted at the knowledge of his own power with God."[62]

[62] *Life and Miracles*, p. 12.

CHAPTER VIII

Devotion of the Popes

WE READ THAT THE CANONIZATION OF SAINTS is intimately connected with the existence of miracles, and it is the common teaching of theologians and canonists that the decree of canonization is infallible. Holy men and women are raised to the altars almost year after year, and this distinction is never given to them unless miracles have been worked in proof of their sanctity.

In former times the Holy Office of the Catholic Church had a more ample jurisdiction over the cause of canonization of a saint, a privilege now reserved for the Sacred Congregation of Rites.

The approbation of the devotion to St. Philomena and the authorization of the public cultus of the Saint by the Holy See were based more on the miracles wrought through her intercession than on the examination of her life, of which nothing was known except her name and the fact of her martyrdom — information disclosed to the world by the discovery of the tomb in the Catacomb of St. Priscilla. "It is worth stressing this case of an unknown raised to the altars, a case unparalleled in the history of the Church," says Henri Ghéon.

The Sacred Congregation of Rites proceeded cautiously, scrutinizing the facts dating back to the exhuming of the relics from the catacomb in 1802, even though popes and princes lavished honors upon her.

Twenty-five years after the discovery of Philomena's body, her cause for canonization actually began. Monsignor Filippo Ludovici, Church Treasurer of the sacred relics in Rome, presented to *Leo XII* a copy of the second edition of Don Francesco's book about Philomena and the wonders of the shrine in Mugnano. That was 1827.

Don Sauveur Pascali, a celebrated missionary who was present, said the Pope rapidly ran over the work and asked questions of Monsignor Ludovici concerning the miracles wrought through the holy Martyr. He appeared impressed with high admiration for her and praised God for the power given her. He blessed, in most affectionate terms, the persons who, under the protection of this Saint (these are his words), consecrated themselves, though in the midst of the world, to the practice of perfection. Leo XII granted permission for altars to be dedicated and chapels to be erected in honor of St. Philomena. This Holy Father proclaimed her the *Great Saint.*[63]

From that time the number of those devoted to St. Philomena was multiplied in the very center of Catholicity. Many received the most signal favors after visiting the shrine.

Italy had been the main theater of the wonders attributed to Philomena's help. There in the very presence of the pillar and seat of truth, orators had preached on the prodigies of the Virgin-Martyr. Books from which they gathered their information had been published and republished. But still Rome was prayerfully slow in proceeding with the canonization of this little maiden of long ago.

Gregory XVI, who instituted investigation regarding the girl martyr, Philomena, was most precautious. He had personally been witness to the miraculous cure of Pauline Marie Jaricot, foundress of the Propagation of the Faith. He had given his apostolic blessing to the invalid long before she was carried on a litter to the shrine of St. Philomena. Pauline had seemed beyond medical help. When she returned from the Mugnano shrine and came in person to present herself at the Roman Tribunal, Gregory XVI declared her cure "a miracle of the first class."[64] This most famous miracle was proclaimed

[63] *Life and Miracles,* p. ix.
[64] Burton, p. 112.

in 1835. Then for two years after he had been convinced of Philomena's miraculous power, the Sovereign Pontiff with characteristic vigilance meditated and prayed before he took the final step in the process of calling Philomena the "Thaumaturga (wonder-worker) of the Nineteenth Century." This Pontiff also gave the Saint the new title of Patroness of the Living Rosary, an association of prayer founded by Pauline Jaricot, in conjunction with the Association for the Propagation of the Faith.[65]

Gregory XVI declared his personal love for the youthful Saint not only by authorizing her cult and elevating her to sainthood. He proved to all his intimate feeling for Philomena by sending to her shrine a magnificent gold and silver lamp. He blessed one of her images, destined to receive public devotion in the capital of Christendom.

On January 30, 1837, the girl, Philomena, was given her place in the sanctoral cycle with a special feast appointed for September 9 — *"in honorem s. Philumenae virginis et martyris"* (see the lessons of this feast in the Roman Breviary).[66]

When the Holy Father decided on this unprecedented canonization he granted the liturgical celebration of her feast with a Mass in her honor. The date was later changed to August 11, in commemoration of the translation of the Saint's body from Rome to Mugnano, where the sanctuary has been erected. (The feast is observed almost universally today.)*

Remarkable was the concern of this splendid Prince of the Church in furthering devotion. In 1839 he allowed Philomena's feast to be kept at Mugnano as a greater double. In January, 1841, he raised it to a double of the second class.

It might be noted here that on June 18, 1930, Pius XI approved an official document asking for the introduction of the cause for Pauline Jaricot's beatification. This official document, citing the miracle worked by St. Philomena in the cure of Pauline, had been drawn up at an earlier date. Pauline Jaricot's cause was scheduled for reconsideration in 1952, the sesquicentennial year of Philomena's discovery underground.

---

[65] Goodman, p. 35.   [66] *Catholic Encyclopedia*, Vol. 12, p. 25.

*The reader should note that this book was first published in 1952. See the Publisher's Preface, page viii. —*Editor.*

Pius IX was the pope who in the first year of his pontificate, 1846, announced the freedom of the press in papal dominions and a liberal education program. He won public praise in America. Prominent persons in civic and religious life lauded his wide outlook and enlightened policy. Men like Horace Greeley, founder of the New York *Tribune,* and James Buchanan, United States Secretary of State, commended him.[67]

Pius IX stands out as a friend of our Blessed Mother. He proclaimed the dogma of the Immaculate Conception, December 8, 1854. Fifteen years later he proposed the definition of papal infallibility at the largest attended synod in the history of the Church. That was the twentieth General Council gathered in the Basilica of St. Peter, December 8, 1869.

This great leader who holds the honor of longest reigning pope (1846–1878) was ever faithful to Philomena, the Saint who came to his aid all through his life. In his boyhood he was refused admission to the training school for the Noble Guard because of his nervous affliction, said to be epilepsy. His mother's prayers to Philomena were answered in heaven's own way. Her boy, Giovanni Maria Ferretti, became the Guardian of Christendom, Father of the Universal Church.

During his reign the hierarchy was restored in the island kingdom of Great Britain (1850). Among the thirty-three Anglican converts in the ministry was Edward Manning, successor to Cardinal Wiseman (1851). For spiritual favors as well as temporal, the Ferretti boy, who became a pope, thanked his benefactress.

His handsome imposing presence dignified the sanctuary of St. Philomena in days when he ruled as Archbishop of Spoleto. He constantly encouraged devotion to her.

St. Philomena's love for Giovanni was manifested to many some years later when he was Archbishop of Imola. The life of the prelate seemed ebbing away. Near his bedside stood a lovely statue of his favorite Philomena. Bystanders declare they

[67] Joseph McSorley, *An Outline History of the Church* (St. Louis, Mo.: B. Herder Book Co., 1943), p. 866.

heard her rap distinctly as she sometimes does when she is about to work some great miracle. Even priests have verified what they call "St. Philomena's knock of assurance." (This statement is a pious belief. It is not an article of faith.) Immediately the patient improved and speedily convalesced.[68]

As Sovereign Pontiff, Pius IX honored the little Saint by a regal visit. He celebrated the holy Sacrifice of the Mass on the altar dedicated to her in the sanctuary of St. Philomena on November 7, 1849.

"After the Mass, Monsignor Ginnava Pasca, Bishop of Nola, handed the Pope the vial containing the blood of the martyr, Philomena. The Holy Father signed his own forehead with the relic, then presented it to the King, Ferdinand II, ruler of the two Sicilies, and his Queen. Thereupon His Holiness and the royal family proceeded down the aisle, seven little princesses and princes trailing color behind them."

The plaque in the sanctuary bears testimony of this visit. Inscribed is the statement that the Pope, Pius IX, blessed the shrine with his presence. Full details are engraved.[69]

Other marks of devotion for his special advocate are recorded. As Pius IX, he immortalized St. Philomena in 1849 when he named her Patroness of the Children of Mary. He declared her to be secondary Patroness of the Kingdom of Naples.

In 1854 the Holy See approved a Proper Mass and Office in her honor. This special privilege is reserved for few. Under such unusual circumstances this permission was rarely granted. Obviously the Pope whose foresight led him to found in Rome the Latin American College in 1853, and the College of the United States of America in 1859, was a wise man. Like the Curé of Ars, this Pope, Pius IX, followed directions outlined by Philomena. "The world is so sure of his sanctity that process for his beatification has long since been proposed."[70]

The last and surest tribute of his personal love for St. Philo-

---

[68] "Annals of 1850–1855."
[69] *Ibid.*
[70] Conde B. Pallen, *The New Catholic Dictionary* (New York: The Universal Knowledge Foundation, 1929), p. 766.

mena was his deathbed remembrance. He had walked through life with her memory in his heart. He walked out of life, leaving his memory over her heart. The pectoral cross that for years hung around Giovanni Ferretti's neck now encircles his "Miracle Saint."

They called *Leo XIII* the "Socialist Pontiff"[*] because he championed the rights of the workingman. His encyclical *Rerum Novarum* has been printed and reprinted. When dying at the age of ninety-four, he composed a sonnet on his approaching death, another mark of his initiative and will power.

Great Leo XIII loved and trusted a little Saint. During his lifetime he showed deep respect for this Saint his predecessors had so honored. Twice, while apostolic administrator of the diocese of Benevento, he made pilgrimages to Mugnano to solicit help from Philomena, special friend of priests, bishops, cardinals, and popes. When he wore the papal crown, he remembered her by sending a gift from the Vatican Exposition to her shrine. This valuable cross is one of Philomena's many presents from the princes of the Church.

Leo XIII was a man with a long-range view. He thought every plan completely through to a finish before he acted and in his mind weighed the possible results. After serious reflection he opened the Vatican Archives and Library for study, dreaming of the day when students from all over the world would profit by the Vatican treasures. He showed his approval for the Confraternity Movement and other institutions in the Church. He set the stamp of highest approval upon the St. Philomena Confraternity by raising it to the rank of *archconfraternity* and enriched it with numerous indulgences. Then he blessed and approved the *Cord* of St. Philomena, attaching special privileges and indulgences to all who wear it.

Nearly fifty years before the consecration of Cardinal Sarto as *Pius X*, now *Blessed*, the Holy See, in 1854, had approved a Proper Mass and Office in honor of the Virgin-Martyr, St. Philomena.

[*]A more proper term would be the "Social Justice Pontiff." Pope Leo XIII wrote an encyclical condemning Socialism. —*Editor.*

As sovereign pontiff he advocated the wearing of the Cord of St. Philomena. He sanctioned the centenary of the cultus of the Saint and granted indulgences to all who participated in commemorating the feast days. "He commanded that all the decisions and declarations of his predecessors concerning Saint Philomena should in nowise be altered. By a Decree of April 3, 1906, Pope Pius X definitely sanctioned the Statutes of the 'Oeuvre de Sainte Philomene,' canonically erected at Rome, to propagate and increase devotion toward the Virgin-Martyr. Finally, that same year, on June 14, the Associates of the Archconfraternity of Saint Philomena and Saint John Baptist Vianney received from the Holy Father the Apostolic Benediction, as well as his wishes for the success of all their works."[71]

There remained for Pius X only personal favors to grant. Priceless tokens of his esteem for the Girl Saint frequently found their way from his palace to her shrine. Giuseppe Sarto's love for poverty was so evident in his constant gifts to the poor that he refrained from wearing jewels. These he accepted only with the mental reservation of bestowing them on some worthy cause. To St. Philomena he dispatched his most expensive ring, an imposing gold band inlaid with topaz. The fact that this little "Saint of the Working Class" wears on her finger the regal ring of a prince is typical of her way with even the saints, for Blessed Pius X, Pope of the Blessed Sacrament, was a saintly man.

Those who conversed with him recall his simple affection for her. Warmth seemed to flow out of the Holy Father's heart while he talked of St. Philomena. Father Paul O'Sullivan remarked this kindliness when he stopped on his way from St. Philomena's shrine to have an audience with the Pope.

[71] Goodman, p. 38.

CHAPTER IX

St. Philomena's Popularity

IN FRANCE

NO POLISHED PROSE OR EXOTIC COLOR is necessary to publicize St. Philomena in France. She herself brings contagious enthusiasm because of her power with God. And she is never outdone in generosity.

As early as 1834, *three years before her canonization*, Philomena was rising to fame. Not drenched with emotion is the story of St. Philomena in a small town in France. It is stark reality.

The Archbishop of Paris gave a small relic of St. Philomena to the church in *Sempigny*, a poor ghost town, close to Noyan. The parish was most grateful. Then a flame caused by a spark from a candle started a fire. The altar, aged and shoddy, seemed beyond hope of preservation. The maddening tongues of fire licked the altar cloth but stopped their feeding within a few inches of the St. Philomena reliquary. The flames encircled the treasure without touching the wood beneath it.

The little parish of Sempigny felt desolate when deprived of its church. Only their faith sustained the people. "If Philomena has no altar, she will provide one for herself," they said. And St. Philomena did not let them down.

How the Saint took affairs into her own hands is just another instance of her executive power. A rich young man found a leaflet about St. Philomena's intercessory power in heaven. He went direct to Sempigny. Imagine his shock when he saw a pile of charred wood instead of a church! Seeing the reliquary of St. Philomena standing on timber blackened by smoke, he determined to build the Saint a shrine more worthy of her bones.

St. Philomena's new friend spent his fortune in building a stone church at Sempigny. The altar and the shrine are of fine marble. The walls of the chapel today are covered with *exvotos,* gifts of those for whom St. Philomena showed her pleasure by obtaining innumerable graces.

From Mrs. Jameson's book on sacred and legendary art[72] comes the assurance that *Paris,* the style shop of the world, took time out to honor the Virgin-Martyr, St. Philomena. In a somewhat perplexed tone the artist, Jameson, remarks: "I did not expect to encounter St. Filomena at Paris; but to my surprise, I found a chapel dedicated to her in the church of Saint Gervais; a statue of her with the flowers, the dart, the scourge, and the anchor under her feet; and two pictures, one surrounded after the antique fashion, with scenes of her life."

Literature preserves a record of things we want to be preserved. Sometimes this literature is written on the fleshy tablets of men's minds and hearts. And then we have tradition.

In written and vocal record the story of the Philomena shrine at the *Church of St. Gervais* is ever new. One of the side chapels is strikingly famous the world over. St. Philomena's power among the people of Paris reaches out to cure the sick and ease the heartsick, to stifle despair and revive hope.

Her miraculous protection saved the church of St. Gervais during the Commune attack. It stood unharmed while all the neighboring village lighted the sky with flames. The Communists outraged the vicinity. They attempted to sack the church of St. Gervais, but the night they came, one of their own band repented and was on the spot to spread the alarm and drive off the cruel horde.

[72] See Chapter XII, pages 130–132.

The revolutionaries entered three times, but each time their efforts failed. They seemed unable to take anything. In desperation they pillaged all the public buildings and set fire to the Hotel de Ville and the Maire. The church where St. Philomena kept vigil remained undisturbed.

Since that memorable time the sanctuary lamps in Philomena's chapel burn throughout the night and day. There are thirteen lamps, symbols of the teen-age martyr, Philomena. The oil from these lamps is believed to have healing power.

While night life rolls on its way in this gay city, there is a little corner where souls may pray. There in the church of St. Gervais the priest intones the evening benediction. Heads bow and petitions go heavenward. Philomena is there in Paris, and she loves it, and she loves especially the Archconfraternity established there in her honor.

Mrs. Jameson continues to speak of shrines in Paris. "In the church of Saint-Merry, at Paris, there is a chapel recently dedicated to 'Ste. Philomene,' the walls covered with a series of frescoes from her legend, painted by Amaury Duval — a very fair imitation of the old Italian style."

In the *Visitation Convent at Nantes* St. Philomena has had a place of honor since the time of Pauline Jaricot's cure in 1835. That a nun in the Visitation Community always carries the name, Philomena, is not surprising. The name is lovingly used in many communities. Every province of the Sisters of Charity throughout the world has a Sister Philomena.

At *Neuville-sur-Seine* the chapel carries the distinction of a labor of love. Philomena's clients built it with their own hands in honor of their Saint.

At *Puget-Ville* in the mountains an old chapel was dedicated to the Saint of Shining Miracles in 1838, just after her canonization the year before.

The shrine of *Thivet,* in northeastern France, has an interesting origin. American boys, who returned from the Battle of the

Marne in World War I, heard the story when they went to Thivet to pray.

A college youth had an appointment with the pious Curé of Ars whose prudent counsel many people sought, but a sudden illness prevented the student from going. The young man determined to carry out the interview by proxy. He asked a priest friend to go in his name to Ars. The delegate promised, but before he arrived in Ars, the Curé died. The priest honored the young man's request by offering Mass at the altar of St. Philomena for Father John Vianney, the holy Curé, and also for the sick student.

Then he visited the Curé's tomb where he thought he heard a voice, directing him to build a shrine to St. Philomena in his own vicinity of Thivet.

The priest acted on the inspiration. He begged a small relic from Pauline Jaricot, who had been specially privileged in carrying a few relics back to France. She unhesitatingly shared her treasure with the priest. Pauline seemed to understand Philomena's desire to have a shrine in the valley of the Marne. Someday that would be a historic site.

The young man recovered as soon as the priest blessed him with the relic. He gave his time and energy, as well as his money, to help with the erection of the shrine of Thivet, a sanctuary of marvels ever since.

In England

The story of Philomena's introduction to England is really the story of Father John Caulfield of the Diocese of Westminster. His bishop assigned him to establish a parish in Pinner, a suburb of London, in December, 1913.

From boyhood days he had prayed to his mother's pet, St. Philomena. He relied on her to help him in this new district. With assurance of heavenly aid he gathered about twenty Catholics. With their help he outfitted a room to serve as a chapel in the vacant house available for use as a rectory.

For the first time since the Reformation the holy Sacrifice of the Mass was offered in Pinner, February, 1914. His small congregation dwindled during the Great War, but Father Caulfield carried on his plan to build.

By October, 1915, his new church was dedicated by the archbishop under the patronage of St. Luke. The new building was debt free, though Father Caulfield started from scratch. He had nothing. Personal friends came to his assistance with funds.

In 1923 Father Caulfield completed the annex to his church, which was a mile away from his rectory. By August, 1926, he had a modern, well-furnished new rectory to harmonize with the church. This presbytery, a silver jubilee gift, was another of St. Philomena's surprises. On the twenty-fifth anniversary of his ordination he received a lovely statue of St. Philomena from his lifelong friend, O'Malley Moore, editor of *Saint Anthony's Annals* in Ireland.

Relics were sent from Mugnano to Pinner in 1930. The following year, 1931, the feast of St. Philomena was solemnly celebrated at the beautiful new shrine. Both the shrine and the majestic altar were entirely free of debt. The Holy Father sent his blessing. From the high commissioner of the Irish Free State came a letter of congratulation. This gentleman became a devout client at the Pinner shrine. The unveiling of a stained-glass window took place on January 10, 1932.

In March, 1933, just twenty years after Father Caulfield had established his parish, he acquired the property adjoining the church grounds. St. Luke's campus was then sizable enough for an outdoor pilgrimage that August.

Down the suburban street of London town went Philomena's relics encased in the English reliquary. Pinner's increasing Catholic population filed prayerfully along. A Jesuit priest preached on the efficacy of the Saint's intercession, calling attention to the landmark she had helped Father Caulfield to set upon the English soil.

The religious element in Pinner is heightened and enlivened by the annual Pinner Derby held for the benefit of the church.

These little Shetland racers have won for the jockeys a fame that naïvely links them with the playful term, "Philomena's ponies."

In Portugal

In a letter of January 27, 1952, Father Paul O'Sullivan in Lisbon has sent direct information regarding St. Philomena shrines in the Spanish Peninsula. It is a pleasure to quote the sincere words of this Dominican priest, whose zeal has carried the Saint's name around the world. He writes:

"The principal Saint Philomena Shrine in this country is in our own church of Santo Corpo. . . . When we started the devotion about thirty years ago the name of our dear little Saint was practically unknown in Portugal or its colonies.

"Now the dear Saint Philomena is not only honored by us but by many. She has made our church the center of devotion for all Portugal and its colonies. Devotion from here has spread to Ireland, Scotland, many parts of Spain, West Indies, and Australia.

"Our little book about Saint Philomena, thanks to the won ders she does wherever the book goes, has gone into thousands of copies. That book has been translated into Portuguese, Spanish, Dutch, Hungarian, and Danish.

"Now there are statues of the Saint in most of the very many churches in Lisbon, and in many of the churches throughout the country. Cards and pictures of our dear little Saint have gone into the millions.

"We celebrate her feast not once a year, but once a month. The church is packed during the services throughout the day and evening. If you wish me to tell you more about Saint Philomena's power for doing good, I can. . . . But you already know that by now."

In Pittsburgh, Pennsylvania

St. Philomena played as active a part in Pittsburgh in 1838–1839 as she did in Italy or France. Certainly the story of the foundation of the Redemptorist priests in America is the story of Philomena's intercessory power. In this instance the Saint won for herself the title of "Mediatrix in Pittsburgh."

The year 1839 stands out also as the year the Redemptorist community could rejoice that their founder, Alphonsus Liguori, was raised to sainthood, just two years after Gregory XVI had canonized Philomena. Perhaps heaven ordained that Redemptorists everywhere have special devotion to the Virgin-Martyr since her crown of glory so closely antedated that of the Redemptorist saint.

It was Philomena whose help Father Joseph Prost invoked to quell a storm at sea when he was crossing from Bavaria to establish a monastery over here. That was early in 1838. Philomena's popularity as a new "Star in Heaven" led him to promise that he would name his first church in her honor if he and his companions landed unharmed. They did. But Father Prost like so many other mortals was slow to fulfill his promise.

For this he cannot be upbraided. Divine Providence has Its own way in working all things unto good.

Who was Father Prost? How does he fit into the picture with Philomena the realist? It is a long story that trails from trouble to triumph. But it is true.

A clear view of Philomena's interest calls for a brush-up of memory to the time when the iron foundries and coal mines of Pittsburgh lured many industrious Germans to establish homes and rear families. Materially they could prosper. Spiritually they starved. Covered-wagon days saw few priests, especially German-speaking priests.

Fort Pitt was established in 1758. Over a period of twenty or thirty years about eighty Catholic families had settled in the district. Some missionary priests had visited, among them the prince-priest, Demetrius Gallitzin, who brought the Faith to the Alleghenies, and Benedictines from Sportsman's Hall, Latrobe.

Early in February, 1839, Father Joseph Prost heard of the orphaned German Catholics in Pittsburgh. At that time Father Prost's community of the Divine Redeemer had been struggling to establish a footing on American soil. New York, other seaboard cities, Virginia, the Midwest, and the West had offered temporary abode, but no lasting foothold. It was in Peru, Ohio, that Father Prost was laboring when Mr. Addlemann, a German farmer from Butler, suggested that the Redemptorist Fathers take over the struggling Germans of Pittsburgh.

To Father Prost this seemed the solution to his community worry. Knowing clerical etiquette, he suggested that Mr. Addlemann inform the Bishop of Philadelphia about the proposal, since an invitation would be in order before even the most zealous religious could assume control of a parish.

Upon receipt of Mr. Addlemann's letter, Bishop Kenrick communicated immediately with Father Prost.

Very Reverend Father:
As I have been informed by a letter sent to me from Pittsburgh that Your Reverence is willing to send there a priest of the Congregation of the Most Holy Redeemer to take charge of the German Catholics who for some months have been without a Pastor, I wish you to know that such action on your part would be very gratifying to me, and I hereby delegate you to extend to him in my name all the faculties which missionaries are accustomed to enjoy in this Diocese or to exercise these faculties yourself if you go there in person. It is also my wish that you hold divine services in Saint Patrick's Church and in no case in the chapel which has been erected in a certain house in the district of Bayardstown.

Devotedly Yours in the Lord,
Philadelphia, March 5, 1839   Francis Patrick Kenrick

Father Prost lost no time in arranging for his Ohio flock and getting on his way to Pittsburgh. He arrived on April 8, 1839. This date marks a milestone because it represents the first American foundation of the Congregation of the Divine Redeemer.

On the second Sunday after Easter, as commissioned by the bishop, he celebrated his first High Mass in St. Patrick's Church. Knowing full well that he had to proceed with extreme caution and prudence, he simply announced to his audience that by order of the bishop he was henceforth charged with pastoral care of their immortal souls.

According to reliable witnesses, Father Prost was a good singer, a distinguished preacher, and altogether a priest of imposing appearance. In a short time he had won the hearts of these parishioners, and all were more than satisfied with his priestly services, his zeal, and his splendid talents. In fact, all the German Catholics of Pittsburgh desired Father Prost to be their parish priest. His fatherly heart longed to unite these good people. His was a delicate position. He feared to lord it over the few stubborn sheep of the flock because they persisted in maintaining a separate chapel. But he had his command from Bishop Kenrick.

Father Prost tried to reconcile the dissenting minds. Sometimes he held public meetings for the men. Sometimes he called private meetings of the most influential in the group that persisted in maintaining the Factory Street church. The majority at St. Patrick's wanted nothing to do with the few who formed the building committee of St. Mary's. There was strife and bitterness that seemed to be sinking deeper into the hearts of the men.

The trouble had been seeded by a disagreement over the stipulated amount to be paid for the rental of the property and furnishings of old St. Patrick's, which Father O'Reilly had leased to the Pittsburgh German Catholics. Formerly St. Patrick's had been everybody's church. Then the Germans predominated, and the other nationalities built St. Paul's which eventually became Pittsburgh's cathedral.

Had the prosperous Germans conceded to the suggestion that they buy outright the property known as St. Patrick's, their harmony and good will might not have disappeared. When opinion divided, two factions arose. Those who favored Father O'Reilly's sensible plan continued to worship at the mother church.

The dissenting group leased a property on the corner of Fourteenth and Factory Street (Liberty). This building had been a cotton factory, owned by Jacob Schneider. The new chapel became popularly known as the "Factory Church." To appease this group, the bishop named it St. Mary's and appointed Father Henry Herzog as pastor. Father Nicholas Balleis, O.S.B., was delegated to St. Patrick's.

Feeling germinated into real trouble when the clubroom under the new Factory Church was opened as a saloon. Bishop Kenrick immediately closed services, forbade any priest to carry on divine worship in the building, and rebuked the young son of Jacob Schneider for his irreligious act. Father Herzog was transferred to Reading, Pennsylvania, and at this same time the Benedictine abbot recalled Father Balleis to Latrobe. It was a sad Christmas. Pittsburgh had no German priest.

This was the situation that faced Father Prost in April, 1839. And this is the people whose hearts St. Philomena conquered, when all hope seemed to be snapping in the good priest's mind. In the moment of anguish Father Prost remembered Philomena, and turned to her to "take over." And that is exactly what St. Philomena did. She always does when people turn to her with trust. But in her own businesslike way she is shrewd enough to exact co-operation. She goes more than halfway when people pray. One of the prayers that seems to be a favorite is the Apostles' Creed.

Father Prost invoked her aid publicly one Sunday afternoon when he was instructing the children. He had been talking about young saints. At the moment he mentioned Philomena's name a thought leaped into his mind. He acted on it, and after interesting the children in the courageous little Virgin-Martyr, he told them to bring their parents the next evening to an open meeting in the neighboring field.

Curiosity, and perhaps that innate longing for peace, summoned the pious Germans to the sunset meeting that memorable August evening. Friend and foe, they came. They listened while Father Prost told them of his voyage to the new world, of the peril at sea and his own providential escape from obvious

The Shrine Church of St. Philomena located in Mugnano, Italy in the diocese of Nola, near Naples. It was to this shrine that the pastor, Don Francesco di Lucia, brought the newly discovered relics of St. Philomena in 1805. Overnight the Shrine became a place of pilgrimage, and signal favors and even miracles were granted through the intercession of St. Philomena.

The Chapel of St. Philomena within the Shrine Church at Mugnano, Italy. As one enters the church and proceeds halfway up the main nave, this chapel is to the left. Above the altar can be seen the papier-mâché figure of St. Philomena, within which is her skeleton.

A close-up view of the papier-mâché figure of St. Philomena made in 1805 to enclose the actual bones of the Saint. Below the pillows can be seen the container which holds her dried crystallized blood. This figure has miraculously shifted position at various times over the years.

The processional reliquary of the Shrine Church of St. Philomena. On the reliquary is a picture of the martyrdom of St. Philomena, surrounded by relics of various saints; the reliquary is used to bless the people on principal feast days in honor of St. Philomena.

A picture of the miraculous statue of Saint Philomena which exuded "manna," a miraculous oil, on August 10, 1823.

Upper left: A picture of Fr. Francesco di Lucia, the priest responsible for securing the relics of St. Philomena from the Vatican and having them enshrined at Mugnano, Italy.

Upper right: A picture of Ven. Pauline Jaricot (1799-1862), foundress of the Society for the Propagation of the Faith and the Association of the Living Rosary. She was a contemporary of the Curé of Ars and received a miraculous cure at St. Philomena's shrine in Mugnano in 1835, after making a pilgrimage there. This miracle moved Pope Gregory XVI to open St. Philomena's cause.

Lower left: The beautiful statue of Our Lady of Grace in the Shrine Church of St. Philomena at Mugnano, Italy. Cast about 1600, this statue was made in honor of Our Lady of Grace because the Shrine Church of St. Philomena was originally called Our Lady of Grace.

shipwreck when he made a promise to St. Philomena. Then because he told her he would name his first church in her honor, it seemed she was pleased. The storm ceased, the ship sailed on, and not one life was lost.

A new strength overpowered Father Prost. He firmly told the Germans there assembled he intended to reorganize them into one parish and name it St. Philomena's. But the condition laid down would be that they unite with him in a solemn novena, and then vow with him that they would work harmoniously on their new church, and never again oppose religious authority.

Gladly they prayed together every evening during the novena. On the last day the entire people formed a solemn procession through the neighborhood, singing hymns and praying aloud, while the children carried the statue of St. Philomena, the new patron of Pittsburgh's Bayardstown.

The people then knelt and, together with Father Prost, all made the vow to keep the peace and build a new church in honor of the new patroness who would be perpetually honored in their congregation. They promised to further and approve whatever Father Prost would suggest for their good.

Through St. Philomena's powerful intercession Father Prost attained all that he had anxiously yearned for. He tried to justify the confidence placed in him by the now trusting people.

Since old St. Patrick's church property was close to the running canal, and also close to a filled-in cemetery, that property was not considered the best for the erection of a new building. This might just as well be left in the name of the trustees, Father reasoned, especially since there was talk of a new diocese to be formed for Pittsburgh when the next Provincial Council met in the not too distant future.

In accord with Father Prost's proposal, the building committee agreed that the Redemptorist priest acquire the property on Factory Street. The entire ground and the buildings could be bought for $15,000, of which $2,000 should be paid at the will of the pastor of the parish within twenty years.

The important question then arose as to whose name would

be signed on the contract. Father Prost knew the good pleasure of the bishop, who had warned him to take possession only in the name of and as a representative of the Congregation of the Divine Redeemer, but for the use of the parish.

For the sake of peace, Father Prost preferred the express consent of the parishioners. He put the question to a vote the following Sunday. The affirmative was almost unanimous. Only five voters objected to the Redemptorist community controlling the parish. With the approbation of Bishop Kenrick the contract of purchase was signed by both pastor and parish, and registered in the public acts of the City of Pittsburgh.

With the help of God and St. Philomena, Father Prost, who had arrived in Pittsburgh April 8, 1839, now had attained his objective. His community could settle permanently, but even more important was the unison of the people. Trustees appointed by him were to participate in holding the church property only insofar as the pastor approved.

A letter from Bishop Kenrick is here quoted because it clinches the fact that St. Philomena had actually established the Redemptorists in Pittsburgh and delegated them to guide the German Catholics to unity.

Philadelphia, Pa., Mar. 10, 1840

Reverend and dearly beloved Father:

I am pleased that Father Tschenhens has come to your aid; and I wish you to grant him all the special and extraordinary priestly faculties. With regard to the Chapel or Church, there is no more difficulty, since the title of this same is now so secure that no layman could ever wrest it from the Congregation. I therefore gladly authorize you to proceed with the solemn dedication according to the directions of the Roman Ritual.

(signed)
Bishop of Philadelphia

Before that permission for solemn dedication came Father Prost had put up a temporary building adjoining the older building on Factory Street. Within eight months he had a new monastery to house the Redemptorists who joined him to form the nucleus of the American community. These priests served the parish in the new free school as well as the remodeled church and helped the German Catholics to build a grand and glorious new church.

On that memorable day when brass bands streamed hymns to heaven and the German town militia gave out a festive report from their guns, the procession got under way.[73]

On a flower-decked float, twenty-four white veiled girls guarded the new statue of St. Philomena, now patroness of their church. She had given these well-intentioned German Catholics the grace to overcome their stubbornness, the humility to help with their own hands and physical energy to build their beautiful new St. Philomena's Church. She had rebuilt the parish on canonical lines. She had the honor of being the first St. Philomena's in America. This beloved Mediator in Pittsburgh has ever since kept the peace she once restored.[74]

It would also seem that St. Philomena had permanently launched on American soil the good Redemptorist priests who have ever since been on God's tour.

At Seton Hill College, Greensburg, Pa.

In this Western Pennsylvania college for women St. Philomena holds sway. Voluntarily the students adorn their rooms with her lovely little statue. They carry the medal and say the chaplet. Many are now wearing the blessed cord.

Recently someone suggested passing out prayer cards and pictures to the Catechism classes taught by Sisters and students from Seton Hill. Now it seems St. Philomena belongs to the Confraternity of Christian Doctrine. Every week there are more requests to take St. Philomena to Sunday School.

Since Christmas, 1952, Seton Hill has an approved organiza-

[73] A. A. Lambing, *Foundation Stones of a Great Diocese,* 2 vols. (Pittsburgh, Pa.: Republic Bank Note Co., 1914), Vol. 1, p. 179.

[74] Information is taken almost verbatim from the earliest annals of St. Philomena's Parish. This manuscript is also the history of the Society of the Most Holy Redeemer in its foundation days in America. Photostats of the manuscript are available in the Reference Department of Seton Hill College, Greensburg, Pennsylvania. Additional source material is the Hundredth Anniversary Book of St. Philomena's Church.

tion known as *St. Philomena's Friends*. It has picked up momentum with remarkable velocity. By the time this story had gone into its second printing the young Girl Saint had decided to enshrine herself deep in the hearts of Seton Hill students and deep in the hills of the campus. The foundation for her shrine is being laid as funds for erecting it daily pour in.

An excavator lent his bulldozer and his workmen in deference to the Virgin. A civil engineer contributed his services in marking off Philomena's Field. An architect drew the plans for the shrine as his gift to the Saint. Several contractors are estimating the cost of a marble shrine without personal profit, each hoping to be the one chosen to erect the throne for the Princess Saint.

The five foot statue in Texas limestone is ready. It was sculptured by Frank Aretz of Pittsburgh. When it is unveiled it will sparkle with a diadem of diamonds and gold, made of the offerings of many who have invoked and received Saint Philomena's aid. One jewel will be testimony of a conversion and a happy married life. Of the many contributions, the most elusive was a cashier's check for five thousand dollars. On the card in which it was enfolded, the anonymous donor had penned the brief message, "To St. Philomena for her new shrine."

The dream of *St. Philomena's Friends* is to see the shrine a reality by May 24, 1954, Feast of Our Lady, Help of Christians, and the anniversary of the day Philomena's tomb was opened.

In Dubuque, Iowa

Devotion to St. Philomena flowers newly every day, in familiar as well as unsuspected places. In others it has been growing for years, without fanfare, but most effectively, and first knowledge of it is a thrill that fortifies conviction. Brother Timothy, of New Melleray Abbey, Dubuque, Iowa, has told the author in a letter of October 3, 1952, of a hundred years' devotion to Philomena in a Cistercian monastery. The following are excerpts from his letter:

"At Mount Melleray Abbey, Cappoquin, County Waterford, Ireland, there is quite a large shrine of Saint Philomena which the community rather proudly claims to be the 'National Shrine.'

"Here at New Melleray we do not pretend to have a shrine but we do have a picture twenty-two by thirty-four inches, depicting Saint Philomena in prison, which is placed on a landing of the stairs on the way to the chapel with a kneeler in front so guests and visitors can pay their respects to the beloved Martyr. On a table in front of the kneeler are two loose leaf folders that contain typed copies of novena prayers. Many visitors as well as the men who come on week-end retreats pray before this picture. The painting was done about five years ago, on a gratis basis, by Sister Mary Gabriel, B.V.M., who was at that time the art director at Clarke College in Dubuque.

"Devotion to Saint Philomena in New Melleray dates back to the very beginning, more than a hundred years. Sometimes during that period, the devotion lagged a little, only to be revived again. It was only during the past five years, however, that any real effort was made to spread devotion to Saint Philomena outside the monastery. During those five years articles of devotion pertaining to Saint Philomena have been sent into every State in the Union, to Washington, D. C., to Guam, Alaska, Canada, Ireland, Italy, India, and to both South and West Africa. These articles include books (*Saint Philomena the Wonderworker*), medals, cords, chaplets, and novena and other prayer leaflets.

"It has been my privilege and pleasure to try at first only in a very small way to make Saint Philomena known to others for more than twenty years. During that time, my relatives, friends, acquaintances, and strangers have received magnificent favors through her intercession.

"New Melleray Abbey is not the only place in or near Dubuque where there is a century old devotion to the holy martyr Philomena. The Sisters of Charity of the Blessed Virgin Mary have a tradition that Saint Philomena appeared to one of Dubuque's pioneers and instructed him as to which land he should claim and hold for the nuns who would come to build their convent at the place designated by her. (*In the Early Days,* by a Sister of Charity, B.V.M.)

"Just across the River Mississippi, a few miles from Dubuque, the Sisters of Saint Dominic at Sinsinawa, Wisconsin, also have devotion to this great Saint going back to their very founding. This devotion was introduced to the Sisters by their founder Father Samuel Mazzuchelli. A few years ago this fact was told me by Reverend Mother Samuel. The Sisters have had a statue of the Saint in their chapel for about sixty years."

In Briggsville, Wisconsin

A hundred years after Wisconsin Territory had been admitted to the Union, Briggsville caught the eye of motorists searching the road maps. And why, of all lake regions, such a sudden interest in Briggsville, a tiny fishing resort with a population of less than three hundred? For the same reason that tourists blaze the trail to other persons of renown.

Briggsville's attraction centers on the shrine of a saint. There in the diocese of Madison, in Marquette County, a self-sacrificing priest devotes his frail energy to calling the world to venerate a Virgin-Martyr, known as St. Philomena.

Like the saintly Curé of Ars, who introduced St. Philomena to nineteenth-century France, Father Ignatius Wiltzius has erected a shrine, so far the only outdoor shrine in America dedicated to the "Wonder-Worker," St. Philomena. Between the parish church of St. Mary Help of Christians, and the rectory, St. Philomena calls the modern world to her feet.

There in the cutover pines of Wisconsin is a first-class relic, also a pure white Carrara marble statue imported from Italy, and all the scenes high-lighting the martyrdom of a virgin's life. The story of the Briggsville shrine is recounted from a personal interview with Father Wiltzius as recently as August 13, 1952.

How did the Wisconsin priest come into possession of such a priceless relic? He frankly admits that it was entrusted to him in 1939 by a Chicago woman, Miss Mary Kenny, whom he had never met. She had evidently received it from her uncle,

Father Maurice Dorney, shortly before his death on December 3, 1939. This pious lady in turn entrusted to Father Wiltzius the precious relic and the authentic, dated August 2, 1937, that her uncle had brought from Naples. It was one of those fragments preserved for distribution at the time the Saint's body was being encased in the waxen image.

Father Wiltzius showed his appreciation for the relic and likewise for the eighteen-inch statue of St. Philomena, another treasure from Miss Mary Kenny, by beginning weekly novena devotions at the little shrine he had improvised in the Church of St. Mary at Pewaukee. The only identity Father Wiltzius had with this good woman, whom he had never met, was through correspondence.

Father's assignment to Pewaukee carried some devotion there, but the capricious young St. Philomena obviously had her penetrating eyes focused on the Wisconsin Dells, a fashionable beauty spot studding the Wisconsin River. So maneuvered the Girl Saint until she "got herself there," or at least not far away. Briggsville is just a fifteen-minute drive, a mere ten miles northeast of Wisconsin Dells.

In her own way of popularizing herself, thereby leading people to pray, St. Philomena made a short stop in Janesville, where she fulfilled another of her many missions. Healing the sick is her favorite kindness. It is not surprising that Father Wiltzius and his relic and statue took up their abode in a Wisconsin hospital. There many broken spirits were uplifted as Father Wiltzius related the adventures of the teen-aged girl who suffered excruciating pain even unto death, and never faltered in her faith. Many were the cures effected by the blessing given while the relic was laid upon the stricken ones.

One of those having a deep-seated faith and love for St. Philomena is a Mrs. W. R., who on the tenth day of August, 1945, met with a serious accident, her right arm having been crushed from the finger tips to her shoulder in a bandage-cutting machine. The arm was all but severed from the body. The chaplain of the hospital (Father Wiltzius) was called and Mrs.

W. R. received the Last Rites of the Church; the relic of St. Philomena also was laid upon her and the special blessing imparted. This was past midnight and hence the feast day of St. Philomena (August 11) had already begun. At this time her eldest son, Patrick, who was hospitalized at Portsmouth, Virginia (also a victim of war), was granted an emergency furlough to be with his mother. When it was seen that she no longer was in danger of death, he returned to Portsmouth, August 15, 1945. On September 7, 1945, Patrick's father received word that his eldest son was critically ill and that one of the family should come at once. Before Mr. W. R. reached Fort Wayne his boy was dead. Mrs. W. R. received the word with great composure for she felt God would compensate her for her loss. Subsequent events proved this to be true. After spending almost four months in the hospital, during which time she had expressed a great desire and prayer that God would give her one more child to take the place of her Patrick, the almost incredible happened. Mrs. W. R. was advanced in years at this time, but on February 9, 1947, there was born to her a perfectly lovely little girl now six years of age, and we may well understand why she was given the name of Philomena in Baptism. Mrs. W. R. is very frequently called upon to speak at women's clubs to tell of the wonders of St. Philomena, "to whom nothing is refused."

Another recovery is that of Floyd D. This young man was afflicted with osteomyelitis and was operated upon several times, but again was scheduled for a similar operation. The evening before this, Father Wiltzius prepared him for the reception of the Sacraments, and also laid upon him the relic of St. Philomena and imparted to him the special blessing. Floyd's cure resulted without an operation. To Floyd and his wife was given the blessing of another child and they named her Philomena.

In Wisconsin just as in Naples St. Philomena again proved herself to be the "Children's Saint." Little Peter B. and his pious parents believe this, you may be sure. Peter is now seven. But Peter's family and friends can recall the day when they feared for Peter. That was the time the child caught his hand in a mangle and burned it up to the shoulder. They feared that the injured arm would need to be amputated. Those who know and love little Peter B. will never forget that hopeful cry for help that went heavenward as Father Wiltzius placed the relic on little Peter's arm and imparted the special blessing.

St. Philomena can date her entry into Briggsville with the coming of Father Wiltzius on the last Sunday of August, 1947. The relic and small statue of St. Philomena were publicly enshrined at the feet of St. Joseph in the Briggsville church, dedicated to our Blessed Mother. Friends of the new pastor supplied the $75 for that first indoor wrought-iron shrine. The shrine was blessed and the relic translated to this new place of honor on May 30, 1948.

Devotion spread. The good priest dreamed of a pretentious sanctuary that would bring honor to his beloved Saint. The dream became a reality. Its fulfillment came when the priest's own father provided the $1,200 needed for an outdoor statue. The generous Mr. Wiltzius, who had spent his life bringing Christ into Christmas greetings by advocating religious cards, died eighteen days before the statue arrived from Italy.

On August 8, 1949, the foundation of the shrine was started. The shrine was planned as a replica of the dungeon where the young Martyr-Saint, Philomena, had suffered and died to preserve her virginity. The upper structure is built of granite from many parts of the world. The red granite, which predominates, is the genuine Montello Stone, from Montello, twenty-five miles distant from Briggsville. Another friend provided the stone as well as the trucking from the quarry.

November and May might be said to have combined in building this modern dungeon for the glorification of a little maiden of long ago. The shrine itself was designed and will in time be embellished by Father Wiltzius himself. The labor of love that carried through to perfection can be credited to a man of seventy-six and a boy of sixteen, two extremes of life.

Old Jacob Wieniecki and young Danny Farrell began to work feverishly and completed the structure by September 1, 1950. At this time the marble statue, six feet and three inches high, still occupied the same southeast corner where it had been placed when it was uncrated and set upright. It would have been almost impossible to move so consequently the walls were built around the image. Because of a badly crippled condition "Old Jake" had to use a cane to support himself, yet strangely enough, after about the fourth day, he discarded his cane and has not used it since. His "little girl friend," as he fondly called St. Philomena, he swears, had fixed him up. All in all, there are over forty-five tons of granite in the superstructure alone, every ounce of which was hauled and laid by "Jake and Danny."

Money for the mortar and the cost of labor (about $974) came from the John O'Keefe estate and a few others. The decorative lighting was supplied and donated by Leo Farrell of Portage (The Midwest Sign Company). Another of the most ardent and generous devotees of the shrine of St. Philomena is Mr. William Dee of Chicago who donated $500 toward the windows, Mr. Weston, the designer and executor, having donated the balance of $750. On many other occasions Mr. Dee has made substantial donations, thus helping the shrine when in dire need.

These five windows, designed by Chester A. Weston of Minneapolis, have a money value of $1,250. Actually they are priceless. Only one who has made a study of genuine stained glass can appreciate the art and effort put into the windows. Every piece of glass that makes up the color combinations has been leaded together, and all shadows and dark solids are painted in with iron oxide and in heating are fused with the glass. It is not merely surface enamel.

The stained-glass windows tell the entire story of the life and tortures of the "beloved" Saint in pictures and symbols. Before them, viewers are at the same time humbled and inspired. There, too, in clear and radiant words, they read and remember to say: "St. Philomena, powerful with God, pray for us."

On Sunday, September 3, 1950, the only outdoor shrine in America honoring St. Philomena was solemnly dedicated by

His Excellency, Bishop William P. O'Connor of Madison. In the course of his sermon, he remarked that he had "seen many larger but none more beautiful than the shrine at Briggsville," and exhorted the gathered crowd, of more than fifteen hundred, to stop when passing and say a little prayer to "the little wonder-worker of our own times." On this occasion also, the marble statue, the only one of its kind in the world, was blessed by the Bishop. He publicly expressed his happiness at having St. Philomena in his diocese and also avowed his great love and devotion for "The Forgotten Martyr" since his childhood.

Once more on Sunday, August 12, 1951, St. Philomena's anniversary day was celebrated with great pomp and joy. The Right Reverend Baldwin Dworschak, abbot of St. John's Abbey and president of St. John's University, Collegeville, Minnesota, conducted the closing exercises of the solemn novena in honor of St. Philomena, with not less than 1200 people present. Abbot Baldwin has been an ardent admirer of the little Saint. In fact, it was Abbot Baldwin who, as an assistant to Father Wiltzius at Pewaukee, did so much in inaugurating and promoting the spread of the devotion to this powerful "Wonder-Worker." In his words he pointed out how this little Saint has ever been an inspiration and aid to him in times of trial and tribulation, and exhorted all to take unto themselves the motto: "To St. Philomena nothing is refused."

Again on Sunday, August 10, 1952, at three o'clock in the afternoon, the Right Reverend Monsignor Edward Kinney, pastor of the cathedral at Madison, Wisconsin, conducted the solemn closing of the third annual novena to the Virgin-Martyr, St. Philomena. The services opened with the clergy and children in procession to the church singing: "On This Day, O Beautiful Mother." Arriving at the church, the clergy knelt before the indoor shrine, there to venerate the true relic of the Saint by kissing it. The procession translated the relic to the outdoor shrine to the singing of the beautiful St. Philomena hymn, "We Praise Thee, Philomena." The relic was placed on a pedestal while Monsignor Kinney blessed the new statues, that of St. John Vianney, better known as the Curé of Ars, and that of Blessed Pius X, Pope of happy memory. In his discourse Monsignor Kinney stressed the point that the saints, all of them, were human beings like ourselves with faults and frailties, but we too can make our shortcomings steppingstones to the life of sainthood to which all have been called.

Children, recovered from polio and other serious mishaps, marched in the procession on St. Philomena's day, the one hundred and fiftieth anniversary of the discovery of her sacred body. In connection with the translation of the relic, three beautiful little girls carried a crown for the figure of the dear little martyr of yore, and throughout the day crowds came to pray at the shrine. When we visited the shrine on August 13, St. Philomena seemed radiantly fresh and lovely in her rose wreath. Vigil lights sparkled in the sun, votive gifts left by the generous visitors, their sacrifice of love for their beloved Saint.

Since the dedication of St. Philomena's shrine at Briggsville on September 3, 1950, thousands have come in pilgrimages and individually, and many marvelous deeds are reported to have been wrought through the powerful intercession of "The Beloved Saint of God."

Everywhere

St. Philomena fascinates all who have the individual pleasure of her acquaintance. These devotees have enshrined her from the hills of Italy to the Arctic shores, across Europe to China and Japan, in Trinidad and Alaska too.

In faraway Aruba, a Dutch island off the coast of Venezuela, fishermen call her their patroness. They trust her power to direct them ashore. She who once braved the Tiber is their heroine. Her anchor is their hope. Every year there is a solemn procession on her August feast day. From Lisbon, Portugal, to the United States, especially in New York and New England, the "Saint of Shining Miracles" is daily more beloved. In Chicago at St. Philomena's Church, the pastor encourages his parish to honor her publicly and privately as well. In Milwaukee a pastor recently said, "Saint Philomena is a great girl." He is one more of Philomena's admirers today.

Lately a representative from a Michigan publishing house stated that requests for prayer cards and leaflets honoring St. Philomena have come from every country in the world except Russia. A Detroit lithographer circulates a booklet, carrying the announcement that copies may be secured free upon request, out of gratitude for favors received through the intercession of this Saint. An agent from another city remarked recently that St. Philomena is taking the world by storm. His religious-goods house can scarcely fill the orders that come daily for her statues, pictures, plaques, medals, and beads.

Communities in all parts of the world spread devotion to St. Philomena. In many chapels and oratories her statue is honored. Of all, the sweet simplicity of one village convent will long be remembered. There in the center of the dining-room table is a small statue of the Saint. In answer to the question of a visiting nun, the superior sincerely said: "We trust Saint Philomena to keep the larder full."

Skeptics and cynics will find no brilliance in the so-called capers of this prankish Girl Saint. Those too sophisticated to accept the Virgin-Martyr, approved by several sovereign pontiffs, will not enjoy her story. But she has distinguished friends outside the faith. When Longfellow, a popular American poet, reached the climax of the tribute he wished to pay Florence Nightingale, he called the poem *Santa Filomena*.

Longfellow traveled in Italy. It is possible that he visited the churches of Pisa. There in the San Francesco chapel, over the altar dedicated to Santa Filomena, he could see the Sabatelli painting. In the art gallery of Milan where the Florentine artist's works are now preserved, he would today see more.

Sabatelli has represented St. Philomena as a beautiful nymph-like figure floating down from heaven attended by two angels. The cherubs bear the lily, the palm, and the javelin. In the foreground underneath are the sick and the maimed who are healed by the Saint's intercession.[75]

Since the word *Filomena* or *Filomela* in Italian refers to a songbird, Longfellow played on the surname of Florence Nightingale, comparing the Italian-born English army nurse to Philomena the Saint. The popular hospital reformer and philanthropist during the Crimean War won for herself the title "Lady With the Lamp."

The fame of Florence Nightingale's benevolence is contemporaneous with the early days of Philomena the Saint in Italy. The similarity of the names, Philomena and Nightingale, paralleled the healing arts of the girls. Longfellow was fascinated. He observed the wonders of Mugnano. He read. He wrote. The first issue of the *Atlantic Monthly* (November, 1857) carried his poem.

Santa Filomena

Whenever a noble deed is wrought,
Whenever is spoken a noble thought,
    Our hearts in glad surprise
    To higher levels rise.

The tidal wave of deeper souls
Into our inmost being rolls
    And lifts us unawares
    Out of all meaner cares.

Honor to those whose words or deeds
Thus help us in our daily needs,
    And by their overflow
    Raise us from what is low!

[75] Luigi Sabatelli (1772–1850), painter and engraver, is an outstanding personage in the history of nineteenth-century Italian art. Beginning his study in his native Florence, he continued it in Rome, Venice, and other cities of Italy. He finally settled in Milan, where he taught art in the Accademia di Brera, and where he and his children, artists like himself, collaborated in various projects. He died in Milan, at the age of seventy-eight.

Thus thought I as by night I read
Of the great army of the dead,
 The trenches cold and damp,
 The starved and frozen camp, —

The wounded from the battle plain
In dreary hospitals of pain,
 The cheerless corridor,
 The cold and stony floor.

Lo! in that house of misery
A lady with a lamp I see
 Pass through the glimmering gloom
 And flit from room to room.

And slow, as in a dream of bliss,
The speechless sufferers turn to kiss
 Her shadow as it falls
 Upon the darkening walls.

As if a door in heaven should be
Opened and then closed suddenly,
 The vision came and went,
 The light shone and was spent.

On England's annals, through the long
Hereafter of her speech and song,
 That light its rays shall cast
 From portals of the past.

A Lady with a Lamp shall stand
In the great history of the land,
 A noble type of good,
 Heroic womanhood.

Nor even shall be wanting here
THE PALM, THE LILY, AND THE SPEAR,
 THE SYMBOLS THAT OF YORE
 SAINT FILOMENA BORE.
    — *H. W. Longfellow*

CHAPTER X

St. Philomena's Marvelous Intervention

IT IS FOR THE CATHOLIC CHURCH TO DECLARE which of these marvels related to St. Philomena are to be regarded as authentic miracles. Yet it was the power of her intercession, more than the knowledge of any details of her life, that influenced the Church in declaring her a saint. Philomena *is* powerful with God, as thousands of her friends the world over would say, and then begin recounting the numerous signs of this fact they themselves have experienced or have seen firsthand.

Following are a few of the stories of St. Philomena's powerful help. They will convince most any reader of her favored position in heaven, and of her concern for people of every place and state in life. It is to be hoped that more readers will think a little upon the strong virtues she practiced so faithfully in her few short years and call upon her for spiritual aid, as well as temporal.

Because she comes to their assistance at just the right time, those who love St. Philomena say there is nothing too trivial or too important to concern her.

There is the story of the Lazarist Father Guida who came to the Mugnano shrine to fulfill an act of gratitude for favors received. Father Guida looked longingly at the image of the young Saint, telling her he had the urge to do missionary work among the poor in foreign lands. The following winter of 1853, he lapsed into delirium in a pneumonia crisis. The priests around were saying the prayers for the dying. Father Guida snapped into consciousness when he had the sensation of a hard knock on his arm and two on his head. He thought he saw St. Philomena robed in golden embroidery over white. She playfully reprimanded him for his faintheartedness, and told him to look up and see what God had prepared for him. Like a child obeying, the priest half-opened his closed eyelids and saw a bishop's miter. Then, wide-eyed, he sprang up, a normal man. His praying brothers scattered to the chapel to give thanks.

The infirmarian teased him when he told the story. The community laughingly called him "the ambitious one who would see a crozier the next time he dreamed." The good wholesome fun of his companions turned to sobersidedness a few months later when Father Guida was appointed to the bishopric of Oria. He told his story to the worshipers at the sanctuary at Mugnano, when he returned after his consecration to make an open pilgrimage and offer Mass on the marble altar at St. Philomena's shrine.

The *restoration of a woman's sight* is recorded through the use of the blessed oil that burned before the shrine of St. Philomena. This is quoted from E. Seton's book, *St. Philomena's Roses.*

"A French woman had recourse to the oil of Saint Philomena. For three years she suffered with a disease of the eyes, and so much pain that she could neither eat nor sleep. The slightest contact with air or light would cause her to scream with pain. The doctor did all in his power for her, but finally pronounced her case absolutely hopeless. The poor woman, having devotion to St. Philomena, commenced a novena in her honor and anointed her eyes with the oil. During the novena, her sufferings increased in intensity and continued until the morning of the ninth day. She had to be helped and guided by her daughter in every step she took in the house. On the last day of the novena the good woman had a Mass celebrated for herself, and after the Mass, on taking off her bandages, her sight was suddenly restored."

From old Italian records we read of the *blind man* who left a valuable ring as an *ex-voto* offering to St. Philomena at her sanctuary in Mugnano. Confident that his prayer would be heard and his sacrifice accepted, he returned to his home. He recovered the full use of his sight.

The *cure of a princess-nun* is attributed to St. Philomena's help. It is one of many cures listed in the "Annals" between 1850 and 1860. The central figure of the cure was a princess of Catania, who had entered a convent in Naples and taken the religious name, Sister Maria Emilia. While still young she became paralyzed and blind. Patiently she suffered and prayed.

On the night of April 21, 1856, she received a heavenly message through a dream. She thought she heard St. Philomena say: "I have come to tell you that Saturday is the Feast of Our Lady of Good Counsel. Your eyes are to be opened, and for this grace you shall give as a votive offering eyes of silver to the statue of the Virgin of Good Counsel in the small corridor of the convent. You shall say it is a miracle."

There was no doubt in the poor nun's mind that if she looked on the light again it would certainly be a miracle. But she was not at all sure whether this was not a mere dream, so she added in words which could be taken in two ways: "We shall see!"

Philomena said to her: "Do you see me?"

"No," said the nun firmly, for seeing in a dream is not having the use of your eyes.

"Don't worry," said Philomena, "for we shall meet again on Saturday."

At Vesper time on April 26, the nun felt her arm grasped and a voice said: "Sister, I am Philomena. Open your eyes." And she squeezed the nun's delicate arm so hard it hurt for the rest of the day. But the nun opened her eyes and saw. Half an hour later she got up and walked. Two days later her speech came back. She prayed aloud.

Recovery from mental illness is a blessing not only to the afflicted person but also to his loved ones. The "Annals" of 1850 present statements either from persons who were miraculously cured or from their families. This one is remarkable.

A demented young man, Don Giovanini Purcaro, a pharmacist from Ariano, had been committed to the Institute of Avirsa, a hospital for the mentally ill. His family took him to the shrine of St. Philomena. On the third day of their novena the young man was completely restored to normal thinking. Public opinion confirmed this miracle, as witnessed August 17, 1849.

A teaching Sister tells of a boy in her classroom. His unpredictable *epileptic seizures* had been a source of concern to all his earlier teachers. This nun, who met the lad in her eighth grade, placed him under the protection of St. Philomena. The first time the boy seemed on the verge of an attack the keen-eyed teacher quickly directed the other students to a new page in their books, while she slipped a relic of St. Philomena into the sick boy's hand. The lad in an instant seemed to recover. Not wishing him to become a sympathy seeker or a parasite, Sister decided to have a private conference with the boy.

The school year ended without any mishaps. The boy learned to love and trust St. Philomena. He still carries her medal and prays to her for relief from the nightmare of torture epilepsy always brings. His improvement is so evident that even skeptics are inclined to use the word, "miracle."

From a grateful husband in Lisbon, Portugal, a doctor received the following letter reprinted from Father O'Sullivan's book.

". . . You have been in my mind a great deal lately and why I have not written to you long ere this to announce the glad tidings of my *wife's entire restoration to health* I cannot understand.

"Your friend and patron, St. Philomena, has been beyond doubt the Wonder-Worker. My dear wife is now free from her head noises, pronounced incurable, sleeplessness, nervous depression and other ailments. Her digestive organs are working perfectly. The transformation commenced on the 25th of February.

"Her troubles had been going on for five years during which she was successively in the hands of seven clever doctors, who, however, could do nothing for her. *St. Philomena's Life* came to us from you. My wife read it at first in a very cursory manner while in bed where she used to spend the greater part of her time. After perusing it superficially she put it on her table and appeared to forget all about it. She took it up again on the morning of the 25th of February, and this time read it with great avidity, so much so, that she could scarcely put it down. Finally she went on her knees and prayed to the Saint to aid her in her great trouble. Every day after that she read a part of the book and always seemed to find something new in it.

"The doctor's visits had ceased for some time. At the end of a fortnight from the date of her prayer she went to her doctor's house. He at first failed to recognise her, so improved had she become.

"Her cure is not only complete. It is solid. I have waited long to tell you. Now I can guarantee the stability of the change. . . ."

Most of the preceding stories are about events of times long past. Here is one of quite recent origin.

Mr. Felix Parisi, son of Andrew, from Giuliano, in Campania, near Naples, asserts that on December 16, 1946, he received this great favor. *Affected by an inguinal rupture* (in the region of the groin), he was quite near to death. An immediate operation seemed necessary. As well as he could he recommended himself to St. Philomena, and put a picture of the Saint on the spot of the rupture. In a short time the trouble disappeared, and Mr. Parisi felt himself completely cured. He came to the sanctuary to thank St. Philomena, and left there a report in his own hand about what had happened. There is visible evidence, as proof of this cure, in the place where the rupture protruded — like a void space.

Protection in accident is another of St. Philomena's powers. Here is the account of a miracle in the Valentino home at Monteforte, Italy, taken from *Life and Miracles*, p. 58.

Gesualdo and his wife Antonia had a little daughter named Rosa Fortunata. When eleven months old this infant slipped from the hands of her nurse and fell from a window to the ground sixty feet below. The fall must have been rapid for the child struck her head against a brick chimney, detached from it several splinters, and then fell upon the pavement. Her mother, who witnessed the terrible accident, cried out, "Good Saint Philomena, this child belongs to you if you save her for me." The father of little Rosa made a similar exclamation in his fright, and ran to the child. He lovingly lifted her in his arms. Neither wound nor bruise was visible.

From the same source, p. 59, comes this account of another child, the son of a surgeon named Elia, who was miraculously preserved from death through a statue of St. Philomena.

Little Giacomo had suffered a broken leg when run down by a carriage. His own father and other fine doctors of Visciano feared that an amputation was inevitable. The wound became gangrenous, and the boy lapsed into a coma. Then a priest entered the sickroom. Exposing the image of St. Philomena for the family to venerate, he knelt to lead them in prayer for their little boy. Giacomo suddenly opened his eyes and reached for the statue of St. Philomena. Every trace of gangrene disappeared. The foot had been cured and the small boy could walk without a limp.

In the old Italian books from Mugnano we read of St. Philomena's *intervention in a planned robbery*.

One morning, as Don Francesco was entering the church at Mugnano to offer Mass he saw his mother run toward him, saying, with an affrighted look, "Give me a moment; I have something to tell you. I feel myself strongly urged to tell it to you." She recounted a dream she had on the preceding night.

She said: "I thought I saw Saint Philomena preparing for a journey. Fearing that she wished to leave us, I begged her to remain. She quieted my fears, by promising she would return the next day. She explained that the Terres family in Naples were exposed to great peril. Gratitude required that she should go to protect them from it."

Don Francesco regarded this dream as a figment of the imagination, but after a little reflection he decided to inform his friends, the Terres.

They received his letter and were astonished to read of an event which had actually taken place the night before.

Robbers, disguised as foreign soldiers, had come for lodging. When the door was not opened for them, they began to force it. They threatened fire and sword. These vandals were on the verge of breaking in. The Terres suddenly realized their personal danger. They implored the help of St. Philomena. "No," they said, "the saint will not abandon us. Let us pray. Let us have confidence in her. We shall be delivered from this danger." Their hope was not in vain.

At the moment the burglars rushed toward the staircase, after forcing the door, the family heard several friendly voices call from without, "Light, light! Quick, quick! Bring us a light!"

These cries, several times repeated, aroused the people of the house, and frightened away the robbers. The Terres family were relieved to see their neighbors rush in. The different circumstances of this event seemed singular to both parties. The mystery was explained the next morning when the letter arrived. The Terres family and their neighbors who, without knowing why, had come to visit so late, discovered the finger of the Saint in what had passed, and thanked her in all the effusion of their hearts.

Saint Philomena is often called the Baby Saint. Replicas of the statue of the Saint and prints from her shrine, as well as medals, have proved efficacious to *expectant mothers*.

There is one instance where the Saint is supposed to have

encouraged a timid wife who might have faced the birth of her child in painful despair. Finding herself alone, she prayed to the Mother of God for help. A maiden appeared by her bedside saying she was "Philomena" sent to assist. The relieved mother-to-be promised to name her child after the kind girl. The baby lived. The heavenly maiden vanished. When the new mother carried her child to the church, she saw a statue of the Virgin-Martyr, Philomena, and recognized its similarity to her heaven-sent helper.

Destitute mothers, especially, seem to find favor with St. Philomena.

At Vista, a town situated at the foot of Mount Gargano, in Italy, there lived the very virtuous, but miserably poor family of Giovanni Troya and his wife, Maria Teresa Bovini. The family had moved to Vista in the hope that they might find better work. A ruined cabin, around which was a small impoverished garden, summed up all their earthly possessions. The view to the future, with an addition to their family, afforded little consolation. On the eve of giving another infant to the world, Maria Teresa was on the verge of despondency.

She had neither a layette for the baby nor enough fuel to warm the house; only her faith sustained her. Confident that God can do all things, and trusting St. Philomena, Maria Teresa prayed to the Saint for help in the hour of need. At last the dreaded time had come, but not the earnestly sought relief. The embarrassment of both the mother and the neighbor who aided her was exceedingly great. Maria Teresa complained with a cry to St. Philomena. The neighbor searched everywhere for a covering for the child but there was nothing to be found. Moved with compassion, the neighbor woman took a scarf from her own shoulders and wrapped the new baby in it. The poor mother, realizing that there was not even a sheet in which to wrap the baby, pointed to an old trunk in the corner. The attending woman ran to open it. To her surprise she saw a little bundle of neat and elegant clothes, arranged with order. A perfume, delicate and sweet, issued from them. She took the treasure and kissed it. The overjoyed mother relaxed, unable to express her gratitude to her heavenly benefactress.

The infant, richly dressed, was soon carried to the church to be baptized. The news of the miracle had traveled quickly around the town of Vista. People came from near and far to kiss the wonderful clothes and to breathe the heavenly perfume. The next night Maria Teresa was awakened by the cries of her baby, and reached for it. The child was not at her side where she had laid it before falling asleep. Terrified, she turned to the other side of the bed. There Maria Teresa saw a young girl dressed in white, and of heavenly beauty, holding the child in her arms. What consolation for the poor mother! Immediately she sensed that Philomena was in the room. With gratitude the mother reached lovingly toward the sweet young girl. The heavenly visitor kissed the child, gently placed it in the mother's arms, and disappeared.

From another source comes the story of a pious Irish lady who was filled with anxiety when expecting her fifth child because her four previous children had been stillborn. She confided her trouble to her sister, who was a Good Shepherd nun, and asked her to pray for her. The nun promised to do so, and invited her sister to join her in a novena to St. Philomena. The mother soon afterward gave birth to a beautiful child which was full of life and strength, and gave it the name of Philomena, as she had promised.

Modern mothers trust St. Philomena to carry their babies through to the baptismal font. Positive proof of this is Philomena Sharon of Pittsburgh, Pennsylvania. This beautiful ten-year-old girl is a direct answer to the prayers of a young couple who longed for the kiss of their own child. They had just momentarily loved and lost their first three babies, and never looked upon the faces of their stillborn infant twins. This fine young couple prayed for a family. Gladly they accepted from a Sister of Charity some medals and prayers honoring St. Philomena. Before a statue of the Saint they burned a vigil light day and night to keep their lovely child. She was a challenge to doctors who feared she would never breathe or her mother would cease to breathe. Both are normal and happy today.

Of many similar stories this one is selected for retelling.

A young English girl had been happily married to a Frenchman for six months when she contracted a serious illness, and the doctors declared it was utterly impossible for her to become a mother, as she so earnestly desired. Hearing of the wonderful cures which had been wrought at Mugnano, her husband took her there, both hoping that she might be cured, but on reaching Naples the young wife became rapidly worse. Still she did not despair, but shutting herself up one day in her own room she fell on her knees and besought St. Philomena to help her. She told the little Saint that, as her condition was hopeless from a human point of view, she put all her confidence in her, and trusted that as she was so powerful in heaven, and so good to all who sought her aid, she would cure her. She also promised that in spite of her sufferings she would visit the Saint at Mugnano the next day, and would ask her not only to restore her to health but to obtain for her the happiness of being a mother, and that she would give her child the name of Philomena and would direct all the yearnings of its young heart to God.

She trustfully offered her prayer the next day at the famous shrine of the Wonder-Worker, and a year later she returned, a happy mother and in perfect health.

St. Philomena does not approve divorce. On several occasions she has recently asserted herself.

One foolish young couple, in their unwillingness to give and take, were letting their marriage go on the rocks. Their Catholic training seemed meaningless. They had gone as far as an attorney's office. The girl's good mother knelt before a statue of St.

Philomena and promised to acknowledge the favor if this marriage would be reblessed instead of broken. Stranger than fiction is truth. Husband and wife drove up to the family home in a blissful mood. They are happier than ever, and they named their first child after the Saint who brought them joy.

In another almost-broken home St. Philomena heard the prayers of a Catholic wife who has since been an ardent believer in the Saint. The non-Catholic husband renounced one side of a triangle love and repented his wrong. Resentful of the outcome, the interfering woman at first threatened unpleasant publicity. The family appealed to St. Philomena and the embittered woman changed her attitude. She realized her evil influence, moved to another city, and has ceased to be a disturbing element. A St. Philomena statue holds an honored place in that home today.

A Catholic man, attracted by a divorced woman, attempted to divorce his own good wife. The case went as far as the final court scene. The family and friends of the couple stormed St. Philomena with prayers. At the last minute the wonder-working Virgin-Martyr proved herself. The man was publicly thwarted and received from the court a final rejection. Now he is coming to his senses and is on the way back to his God.

A Catholic mother had left her family. For days the children and the father fretted. Neighbors started a novena in honor of St. Philomena. The Sunday before Christmas the mother appeared at the Communion rail with her husband and children. Her brainstorm had passed away. All were happily reunited in her home.

St. Philomena is powerful in her intercession for the *conversion of sinners*. One man was persuaded by his friends to join in a public novena to the Saint. He had not frequented the Sacraments for thirty-four years, but on August 10, the last day of the Novena, he made his confession and shortly afterward received Holy Communion in thanksgiving at the altar of St. Philomena in Mugnano.

Real estate is also in St. Philomena's line. A lady in Pittsburgh is on the verge of becoming a Catholic since she has become interested in St. Philomena's power.

This woman of no special denomination mentioned to one of her Catholic customers the anxiety she encountered because of crowded conditions in her store. She gladly accepted a picture and a prayer honoring St. Philomena, assuring the Catholic customer she would "try out a saint," since no agency had found her a suitable property. Before a week passed the excited unbeliever announced that Philomena must have a "pull" with the Lord of heaven's mansions, because an ideal lot for parking, a storeroom, and an adjoining house came within range of the storekeeper's purse.

Philomena goes all out to help when folks are grateful. In this case the non-Catholic who prayed sold her undesirable property at a profit. When she asked how to thank a saint, her Catholic friend suggested a Mass offering or a gift to a needy child. Ever since the woman has outfitted a small girl on First Communion Day in a nearby Catholic church.

There was once a cleric, known to this author, who is a strong man today, an outstanding professor priest. His every word is forceful. His lectures are attractive and in good taste. He has the ability to direct his drama class to plan carefully and execute simply. Nothing is ever too much trouble for him if it will create or continue good will.

But at the bar of public opinion this outstanding clergyman was not always accepted for his showmanship. There was a day when he could spend his boyhood hours fiddling. He rode the crest of popularity when it came to clowning with his young pals, but with the faculty in most areas of knowledge the young cleric drifted daily into the background. He did not give to his professors the genuine co-operation essential for a college man. Certainly his was not the proper approach to the priesthood. It took the trigger word "flunk" to knock nonsense out of his head, and inject a scare at the same time.

The prefect of studies called a halt. He prudently warned the cleric that he must seek another field. A religious vocation is only for the man who can measure up in zeal, self-sacrifice, and study. The cleric pleaded, and then he prayed. He suddenly remembered something about a young Girl Saint, who rescued students sinking in a deluge of unprepared studies. He recalled also that his mother had brought him a statue of the Saint. Because he had been so carefree, he had not opened the package. Now he had a flight of fancy. He would win over this so-called wonder Saint. Obviously, he did.

He unwrapped the statue, dusted a space for it on his bookcase, then knelt and offered a prayer in petition for St. Philomena's intercession. He promised her he would daily invoke her help, and would encourage other seminarians to show their trust in prayer. That young cleric persevered. His grades improved as soon as he resumed interest in his work.

Today he is one of St. Philomena's best advocates. He wears her cord and her medal always and carries her chaplet. Friends of this learned priest revere his devotion to duty, and they also revere the one he credits with saving his vocation. That one is Philomena, friend of priests — and of hard-pressed students.

From Lisbon, Portugal, comes a letter written in 1951 by a woman who claims a miraculous cure through the intercession of St. Philomena. The writer is Mrs. Marie do Ceu Mendes Raimundo. The following facts from her letter are given in much detail to show the reader, as a climax to this chapter, the care that is taken, more often than not, to keep the facts straight in an account of St. Philomena's marvelous intervention.

Before Christmas, 1939, violent pain interfered with Mrs. Raimundo's walking. Kidney specialists concluded she had rheumatism. Three doctors failed to relieve her. They were concerned to an alarming degree in March when their patient informed them of her pregnancy. They seemed certain that she could not carry the child through to a safe delivery.

The sick woman persisted in going to church where she

received Holy Communion, then prayed for strength to preserve her child for baptism. Though bent in pain she cried:
"Lord, I am all Yours. I offer You my health, my life, and the
child You are giving me. Do not permit it to be destroyed."

She says she returned home with renewed determination to
oppose the doctors' advice regarding an operation. For several
months she suffered acutely from progressive gravid pain. In
December, 1940, her lovely, normal baby was born. Until that
moment doctors and nurses had held little hope for mother or
child.

After the Caesarian birth, the patient complained of severe
pain in chest and ribs. Her walking was definitely impaired.
Another specialist called in on the case diagnosed it as humoral
disequilibrium and performed the autosanguis transfusion.

In June, 1941, a series of bath treatments began at Caldas
Sanitarium. By mid-September of 1942 Mrs. Raimundo had lost
much of her power of locomotion. Her pain intensified.

She failed to respond to another series of treatments at San
Paula Sanitarium in Marvao. Doctors admitted they were baffled.
Radiograms of her vertebral column led them to think several
glands were nonfunctioning.

From Christmas, 1942, until the next Easter Mrs. Raimundo
was under observation at a Lisbon hospital where all medication
failed to relieve her.

Then her first doctor came back on the case and ordered
galvanic currents and diathermal treatment. The suffering
woman was losing hope when a priest offered Mass in her home
for her and suggested that all her relatives and friends unite in
a novena in honor of St. Philomena.

That was November 13, 1943. The next day Dr. Luiz de
Noura called at the home of Mrs. Raimundo while on his way
to a hunting party. Dr. Noura had some time previously with-
drawn his services as a physician because he felt unable to cope
with the malady. He continued his interest as a friend, and
promised to keep alert for any findings in the case. Up to this
point he had done much research but admitted no enlighten-

ment. His long-time friendship with the family intensified his concern.

The next week the sick woman's husband went to Oporto to interview a specialist recently renowned for helping arthritic patients. With confidence in his old family friend, Dr. Noura, he called first at his office to get his professional estimate regarding the competence of the popular rheumatism specialist in Oporto.

After listening to Mr. Raimundo's petition, this same Dr. Noura, who just a week before had seemed at sea, suddenly reached the conclusion that the suffering woman might have osteomalacia, a bone disease. He promised to investigate.

Instead of consulting the specialist in Oporto, Mr. Raimundo returned home to tell his sick wife about Dr. Noura's latest diagnosis and of his promise to visit about December 1, as a guest, and also with another shooting match in view.

The dilemma now was how to get two doctors together in a professional way, since Dr. Sampaio was the attending physician at the Raimundo home. The sick woman invoked the wonder-working St. Philomena to bring about a casual meeting of these two fine medical minds without offending professional etiquette.

The same evening that Dr. Noura arrived, the family receptionist announced Dr. Sampaio as a caller. Mrs. Raimundo immediately realized the heavenly intervention. Impulsively she said: "It is St. Philomena who has brought you together." To which Dr. Sampaio replied: "It is an interesting coincidence." And Dr. Noura added: "This will make an impression on Catholics."

The two doctors held a conference and reached the conclusion that chronic osteomalacia might be the answer to their question. They arranged for the patient to be removed on a stretcher in a Red Cross ambulance to a hospital in Lisbon. There Dr. Ayres de Sousa planned to do a series of radiographs early in January, 1945. *Conclusion:* Osteomalacia, with manifold complications.

January 8, Dr. Polido Valente read the radiographs and reports. After a conference with Dr. Noura (at that time visiting physician), Dr. Valente examined Mrs. Raimundo. Then he held another conference with Dr. Noura. Together they decided to inform Mr. Raimundo.

"It is better to be frank with the husband," said Dr. Noura.

Dr. Valente added: "Yes, the malady is extremely serious and the therapeutics extremely poor. We know what the disease is, but we do not know how to treat it."

Mr. Raimundo, much distressed about his wife's illness, asked: "Is there nobody anywhere who could cure it?"

The professor, Dr. Valente, answered: "No, your wife is a hopeless case."

"But, doctor, have you ever had a similar case in your life?" Mr. Raimundo asked.

"Yes, several in hospitals, but all of them fatal," replied the doctor.

Three days of severe coughing during an attack of influenza fractured three of Mrs. Raimundo's ribs. Dr. Noura confirmed this and ordered the patient to be bandaged, but the intolerable pain necessitated the removal of the bandages.

By January 23 Mrs. Raimundo seemed critically ill. The husband and family realized that only prayer could save her. They called on the parish priest of Benavile and all his parishioners to join them in a novena invoking the miraculous intervention of St. Philomena. The Sisters of St. Louis and nuns from several cloisters united their prayers. The Missionaries of Mary urged all their catechists to pray.

The day the novena ended the sick woman decided she would test the efficacy of all these invocations to St. Philomena. She requested her daughter to help her out of bed. By supporting herself on the bed table, the patient stood, with the aid of her husband and daughter. This inspired enough confidence to fire her with the desire to take a step or two. Her joy was heartwarming when she walked with her guides to the next room to salute her beloved picture of the Sacred Heart. This first attempt to move her feet on the floor restored her sense of balance. Six years' invalidism had severely depressed this woman who had formerly been among the socially prominent of Lisbon.

At the beginning of February the family began another novena, this time with a note of thanks to St. Philomena who seemed to be listening to their prayers. The day it ended, Mrs. Raimundo sent her daughter to the church of Corpo Santo to ask Father Paul O'Sullivan, a Dominican priest, for the use of his relic of the wonder-working St. Philomena. This zealous missionary had been spreading devotion all over the world since his return from a nine-day visit at the sanctuary of St. Philomena in Mugnano. He had witnessed miracles, so he could sincerely tell what he knew to be the exact truth. His writings have led thousands to call on St. Philomena for help in many situations.

When the daughter hesitated because she had not met Father Paul, the girl's mother prophetically told her that St. Philomena would arrange the introduction if it suited her to do just that. Mrs. Raimundo had read about the "capers" of this young Saint.

Sure enough, when the Raimundo girl reached the church, she met an old friend of the family. This lady was delighted to introduce the girl to the priest, and put in her own request for the precious relic to be sent to Mrs. Raimundo.

Father Paul promised the relic within two days. By then he hoped to have it back from another patient. There is always someone waiting to borrow it.

Mrs. Raimundo's turn came. During the time she held the reliquary containing a small bone of St. Philomena, the sick woman said she experienced a supernatural joy and renewed courage to report on February 16 for the basal metabolism test at St. Joseph's Hospital.

The day before the scheduled appointment with Dr. Mendonca Santos, the sick woman again sent her daughter to Corpo Santo Church to ask Father Paul to bring her Holy Communion and to bless her with the relic of St. Philomena.

His answer was: "Take the relic to your mother again. Tell her she may come tomorrow morning at 8:30. She may remain in the ambulance at the door of the church. We shall administer to her without permitting her to lose energy."

On the morning of February 16 the ambulance arrived at the

Raimundo home at 8:45. It was after nine when the ambulance reached the church. A priest brought the Blessed Sacrament to Mrs. Raimundo in the ambulance. Then he blessed her with the relic which she had had in her possession for the past twenty-four hours.

Mrs. Raimundo claims that her torturing pain immediately disappeared and a strange sensation like the coldness of ether seemed to pass through her bones. She had the desire to be absolutely quiet. Her intense stillness and sudden relaxation frightened her husband and her daughter, riding beside her in the ambulance.

At the hospital, Dr. Santos ordered the basal metabolism test to be given while the patient remained on the stretcher to conserve every fraction of her chance to live.

When the analyst, Dr. Costa, reported the calculations, he said in amazement: "It is extraordinary. What a great reaction has taken place in your organism! It is as well as mine."

Another physician said: "Perhaps it was the three drops of Vigantol we administered on the eleventh."

Dr. Santos replied: "No medicine whatever could do that. It could be only a reaction in the organism, which at the present is inexplicable."

The stretcher-bearers who had carried her to the same radiologist for the original radiograms knew about her critical condition then. Now they were astonished, especially when Mrs. Raimundo informed the radiologist that further X rays were unnecessary. He persisted in having more plates because of his vital interest. The patient acceded to his request.

On March 23 Mrs. Raimundo returned to the radiologist for a check-up. After being convinced that his patient felt no pain in any part of her body where he tested by using pressure, he reported that, while the signs of former breakage persisted in the patient, the bones themselves showed a greater density than before, a sure sign of recalcification.

On February 26 Father Paul had started a novena of Masses in thanksgiving, and for the complete cure of the woman so much improved by then. It is to be noted that Mrs. Raimundo had regained the power to walk with the aid of support.

On March 8 Father Paul again visited Mrs. Raimundo, prayed over her, and blessed her with the first-class relic of St. Philomena. Strange to admit, the sick woman had a temporary relapse, in which she felt she was becoming a complete paralytic. Obviously St. Philomena was testing her faith, and calling for more prayers.

Mrs. Raimundo prayed out loud: "Dear little Saint, in the most holy Name of Jesus, do not forsake me in this way. What will my husband say? What will my friends say? I am resigned to everything our Lord sends me, but others know I have trusted in your power. Please help me!"

She says she prayed herself to sleep and was awakened by a loud knock. New life had suddenly seemed to revive her. Impulsively she got up without effort. Her heart rejoiced. When her husband and son arrived from their office they were surprised to see Mother on her feet. And when she walked around the room without assistance, they ran to telephone the good news to Dr. Santos.

The physician refused to credit the news. His answer was: "That is not possible . . . I will come and see for myself."

When Mrs. Raimundo walked downstairs to greet him and proved to him that she could kneel and then stand without pain, he replied: "When the alms is so large, the beggar becomes distrustful."

On April 3 Mrs. Raimundo walked to the office of Dr. Polido Valente, the one who had read her death sentence to her husband. His greeting was sincere, and his verification of the radiograms minute. He compared the first with the second, then the second and the third. After feeling the patient's bones, he shook his head and said: "Very well, very well!" He listened to the story of the novena and blessing with the relic of St. Philomena. Not once did he attribute the cure to any earthly power.

Scores of doctors have since examined these radiograms. All have expressed astonishment at the suddenness of the cure.

CHAPTER XI

St. Philomena Devotions

BETWEEN "DEVOTION" AND "DEVOTIONS" THERE EXISTS A FINE SHADE OF DIFFERENCE. *Devotion* is defined as religious fervor or piety. To the Catholic mind the word *devotions* implies prayers or supplications, especially as designed for private worship. For a century and a half the world has practiced devotions honoring St. Philomena. One of these many forms of expressing love for her is by the recitation of her chaplet. The word *chaplet* is a general name for the rosary said with the help of beads. It literally means a wreath or crown.

The *Chaplet of St. Philomena* consists of thirteen small red beads and three large white beads with a crucifix and a medal of St. Philomena attached. The small red beads are symbolic. Thirteen refers to the age of the girl and red connotes martyrdom. The three white beads symbolize purity. Three refers to the Blessed Trinity. The Apostles' Creed is said on the crucifix to beg the gift of faith. *Pater Nosters* are said on the white beads. On the small red beads the following official prayers are said:

Hail, O Holy St. Philomena, whom I acknowledge, after Mary, as my advocate with the Divine Spouse; intercede for me now and at the hour of my death.

St. Philomena, beloved daughter of Jesus and Mary, pray for us who have recourse to thee. Amen.

On the medal say:
Hail, O Illustrious St. Philomena, who so courageously shed

your blood for Christ; I bless the Lord for all the graces He has bestowed upon thee, during thy life, and especially at thy death; I praise and glorify Him for the honor and power with which He has crowned thee, and I beg thee to obtain for me from God the graces I ask through thy intercession. Amen.

A *novena* or nine-day prayer honoring St. Philomena is not restricted to any set form of prayer. Many approved novena prayers are available. For convenience one is printed in this book. An age-old custom is to recite the Creed and the *Gloria* three times in honor of the triune God, the Father, Son, and Holy Ghost.

A *pilgrimage* is a journey to a sacred place undertaken as an act of religious devotion to venerate a saint or to ask fulfillment of some need, or as an act of penance or retribution. The principal places to which pilgrimages are made nowadays are Rome, Jerusalem and the Holy Places, Lourdes, the Holy House of Loreto, Bruges, Paray-le-Monial, Lisieux, and Fatima. Popular since 1805, the sanctuary of St. Philomena in Mugnano near Naples attracts pilgrims from all over the world. In America pilgrimages in her honor are new. The latest are those going to the Shrine of St. Philomena in Briggsville, Wisconsin, close to the Dells, a world-famous summer resort.

The use of *oil* for anointing is an apostolic injunction (James 5:14). From the Jewish and primitive Church it has stood for strength, sweetness, and spiritual activity. Pure olive oil is used for the Oil of Catechumens and the Oil of the Sick. It is also an ingredient of Holy Chrism. Olive oil is prescribed to be burned in sanctuary lamps, but if it cannot be obtained, vegetable oil is permissible. For lamps burning before a saint's shrine, any vegetable oil will do.

Frequently oil burned at the shrine of St. Philomena has restored sight to the blind, hearing to the deaf, speech to the inarticulate, and the power of using lifeless limbs.

Oil from the lamp that burns constantly before the statue of St. Philomena in St. Gervais Church, Paris, goes out to many parts of the world. Pilgrims carry it with them and post offices are accustomed to handling it.

In the United States many tiny bottles of St. Philomena's oil are mailed out from St. Anthony's Welfare Centre in New York. This oil can also be obtained from the Shrine of St. Philomena, Briggsville, Wisconsin.*

In the early Church virgins wore a cincture or *cord* as a sign and emblem of purity. That is why the cord has always been considered a symbol of chastity as well as mortification and humility. The wearing of a cord or cincture in honor of a saint is of very ancient origin, and we find the first mention of it in the life of St. Monica. In the Middle Ages cinctures were also worn by the faithful in honor of saints, though no confraternities were formally established, and the wearing of a cincture in honor of St. Michael was general throughout France. Later on, ecclesiastical authority set apart special formulae for the blessing of cinctures in honor of the Most Precious Blood, our Lady, St. Francis of Paul, and St. Philomena.

This extraordinary privilege of a cord is shared with still other saints, such as, St. Francis of Assisi, St. Thomas Aquinas, and St. Joseph.

The devotion of the *Cord of St. Philomena* was adopted on account of the innumerable graces obtained through the intercession of the Hidden Saint of the Catacombs. This Cord was first distributed by the saintly Curé of Ars, himself. It was the illustrious Leo XIII who blessed and approved the Cord and attached many privileges and indulgences to its wearing.[76]*

Many records tell of the favors granted to those who wear the Cord. We read of striking cures; for instance, when wound about diseased limbs, the Cord has driven out the pain and healed them. There is also the story of the child who fell into

[76] Ferdinand Heckmann, "Confraternities of the Cord," *Catholic Encyclopedia*, Vol. IV (New York: The Encyclopedia Press, 1913), p. 357.

*Today the reader should write to the National Center for St. Philomena, 5013 Harbor Light Drive, Dickinson, Texas 77539. —*Editor.*

a pool of water, but was preserved because of the Cord of St. Philomena around his waist. The Cord itself remained perfectly dry.

Rules for the Cord

1. The Cord approved by the Sacred Congregation in honor of St. Philomena ought to be made of linen, wool, or cotton, of a white and red color, with two knots at one end to honor her double title of virgin and martyr.

2. It is worn under the dress as a girdle. No ceremony is required in conferring it, but it should be blessed beforehand, and passed or sent by one person to another. When worn out, the new Cord also must be blessed. Children, however young, may receive the Cord.

3. In putting on the Cord, everyone ought to propose to himself constantly to honor St. Philomena, in order to merit her protection against all evils of soul and body, and also to obtain, through her intercession, perfect chastity, the spirit of faith so necessary in the unhappy times in which we live, and the grace of doing violence to oneself so as to lead a Christian life.

4. Those who wear the Cord are counseled to say every day the following prayer:

O Saint Philomena, virgin and martyr, pray for us that, through thy powerful intercession, we may obtain that purity of mind and heart which leads to the perfect love of God. Amen.

Leo XIII, by a rescript dated March 14, 1893, granted 100 days' indulgence to the faithful who wear the Cord of St. Philomena, and recite the foregoing prayer with devotion and contrition.

Plenary Indulgences

1. On the day on which the Cord is worn for the first time.
2. On May 25, the anniversary of the discovery of the body

of St. Philomena in the catacomb of St. Priscilla.

3. On August 11, feast† of St. Philomena.

4. On December 15, the anniversary of the approbation of the Cord by the Holy See.

5. At the moment of death, under the ordinary conditions.

N.B. To gain these indulgences (except No. 5), one ought to go to confession and Communion, visit some church, and pray there for some time for the intentions of the Sovereign Pontiff.

† Another feast, that of her patronage, is celebrated on the Sunday within the octave of the Ascension.

Partial Indulgences*

Seven years and seven quarantines (periods of forty days) on the Sunday which immediately follows the Ember Days of Lent, Pentecost, September, and Advent.

N.B. To gain these indulgences, one ought to be at least contrite of heart, to visit some church, and to pray there for some time for the intentions of the Sovereign Pontiff.

PRAYER ON PUTTING ON THE CORD

O Saint Philomena, who hast endured death for the sake of Jesus Christ, graciously obtain for me patience in this illness, and if it is the will of God, grant that on putting on this Cord, blessed in thy honor, I may recover health of body, in order to labor with greater fervor for the sanctification of my soul. Amen.

NOVENA PRAYER TO ST. PHILOMENA

Illustrious Virgin and Martyr, St. Philomena, behold me prostrate before the throne whereon it has pleased the Most Holy Trinity to set thee. Full of confidence in thy protection, I entreat thee to intercede for me with God. Ah! from the heights of Heaven deign to cast a glance upon thy humble client. Spouse of Christ, sustain me in suffering, fortify me in temptation, protect me in the dangers surrounding me, obtain for me the graces necessary to me, and in particular . . . Above all, assist me at the hour of my death. Amen.

St. Philomena, powerful with God — Pray for us.

*These indulgences would appear to have been abrogated by the new regulations on indulgences. (*Enchiridion Indulgentiarum,* 1968). See the *Enchiridion of Indulgences—Norms and Grants* (Wm. T. Barry, C.SS.R., Trans., Catholic Book Publishing Co., New York, N.Y., 1969). —*Editor.*

CHAPTER XII

Revelations and Attestations

NOTE: *These revelations have received the Imprimatur of the Holy Office, insofar as they are free from anything contrary to faith. The Church makes no further pronouncement. The printing received the sanction of the Holy Office on December 21, 1883.*

1. THE NUN'S TALE[77]

It was August, 1833. Mother Luisa di Gesu, a Dominican tertiary, was at prayer. She looked most longingly at her statue of St. Philomena and her thoughts went fluttery, butterflying as the thoughts of even nuns' minds sometimes do. Although Mother Luisa had probably soared to the heights of mental prayer, in her humility she accused herself of distraction at meditation.

The truth is Mother Luisa was thinking about St. Philomena. The questions popping in Mother Luisa's mind just had to be answered so that she could pray with more conviction.

Not that Mother Luisa doubted Philomena's sanctity. Heaven forbid! All Italy was excited about the unusual favors this young Virgin-Martyr had granted. People were calling Philomena a miracle worker. Mother Luisa had actually interested herself in trying to discover the background of Philomena. Being the author of several books, the writing of one more would be just another research hobby for the nun. What a pleasing topic for a biography this Philomena would be!

From the statue Mother Luisa thought she heard an answer to the question at that moment in her head. "My dear sister,

[77] Don Francesco di Lucia, *op. cit.*

it was on the tenth of August that I died in order to live, and that I entered triumphantly into heaven, where my divine Spouse put me in possession of those everlasting joys which cannot be comprehended by the understanding of man. For this reason His admirable wisdom so disposed the circumstances of my translation to Mugnano. Despite the plans arranged by the priest who had obtained my mortal remains, I arrived in that town, not on the fifth of August, but on the tenth; and not to be placed with little solemnity in the oratory of his house, as he also wished, but in the church, where they venerate me, in the midst of universal acclamations of joy, accompanied by miraculous circumstances."

Fearing she might be under an illusion, Mother Luisa intensified her prayer life. She obtained permission to observe rigorous fasts. She also penanced herself in every thinkable manner without injuring her health. Her directors enjoined absolute silence on her part, advising her to refrain from discussing the revelation or trying to recall it. This test of her obedience proved the sincerity of the nun.

Her superioress wrote to Don Francesco di Lucia asking his advice on the subject, praying him to answer at once several questions regarding the revelations. He responded that they were perfectly in accordance with the facts concerning the shrine, which Mother Luisa had not seen. This reply not only consoled the agitated nun, but encouraged her directors, for the glory of God and St. Philomena, to take advantage of the means the Saint herself seemed to point out, in order to acquire circumstantial information concerning her life and martyrdom. They commanded the nun to use for this purpose the most earnest solicitation with the Saint.

Obedience is always victorious. One day, when Mother Luisa was praying to obtain this favor, her eyes closed as before, in spite of resistance. She heard the same voice, which said to her:

"My dear sister, I am the daughter of a prince who governed a small state in Greece. My mother was also of royal blood. My parents were without children. They were idolaters. They continually offered sacrifices and prayers to their false gods. A doctor from Rome, named Publius, lived in the palace in the service of my father. This doctor professed Christianity. Seeing the affliction of my parents, by the impulse of the Holy Ghost, he spoke to them of Christianity and promised to pray for them if they consented to receive baptism. The grace which accompanied his words enlightened their understanding, and triumphed over their will. They became Christians, and obtained the long-desired happiness that Publius had assured them as the reward of their conversion.

"At the moment of my birth they gave me the name of Lumena, in allusion to the light of faith, of which I had been, as it were, the fruit. The day of my baptism they called me Filumena, or daughter of light (*filia luminis*), because on that day I was born to the faith. The affection which my parents bore me was so great that they would have me always with them. It was on this account that they took me to Rome, on a journey that my father was obliged to make on the occasion of an unjust war with which he was threatened by the haughty Diocletian. I was then thirteen years old. On our arrival in the capitol of the world, we proceeded to the palace of the emperor, and were admitted for an audience.

"As soon as Diocletian saw me his eyes were fixed upon me. He appeared to be prepossessed in this manner during the entire time that my father was stating with animated feelings everything that could serve for his defense. As soon as Father had ceased to speak, the emperor desired him to be disturbed no longer, to banish all fear, to think only of living in happiness. These are the emperor's words: 'I shall place at your disposal all the force of the empire. I ask only one thing, that is, the hand of your daughter.'

"My father, dazzled with an honor he was far from expecting, willingly acceded on the spot to the proposal of the emperor.

"When we returned to our own dwelling, Father and Mother did all they could to induce me to yield to Diocletian's wishes, and to theirs. I cried: 'Do you wish that for the love of a man

I should break the promise I have made to Jesus Christ? My virginity belongs to Him. I can no longer dispose of it.'

" 'But you were young then, too young,' answered my father, 'to form such an engagement.' He joined the most terrible threats to the command that he gave me to accept the hand of Diocletian.

"The grace of my God rendered me invincible. My father, not being able to make the emperor relent, in order to disengage himself from the promise he had given, was obliged by Diocletian to bring me to the imperial chamber.

"I had to withstand for some time beforehand a new attack from my father's anger. My mother, uniting her efforts to his, endeavored to conquer my resolution. Caresses, threats, everything was employed to reduce me to compliance. At last I saw both of my parents fall at my knees, and say to me with tears in their eyes, 'My child, have pity on thy father, thy mother, thy country, our country, our subjects.'

" 'No, no!' I answered them. 'My virginity which I have vowed to God comes before everything; before you, before my country! My kingdom is heaven.'

"My words plunged them into despair, and they brought me before the emperor, who, on his part, did all in his power to win me; but his promises, his allurements, his threats, were equally useless. He then got into a violent fit of anger and, influenced by the devil, had me cast into one of the prisons of the palace, where I was loaded with chains. Thinking that pain and shame would weaken the courage with which my divine Spouse inspired me, he came to see me every day.

"After several days the emperor issued an order for my chains to be loosed that I might take a small portion of bread and water. He renewed his attacks, some of which, if not for the grace of God, would have been fatal to purity. The defeats which he always experienced were for me the preludes to new tortures. Prayer supported me. I ceased not to recommend myself to Jesus, and His most pure Mother. My captivity lasted thirty-seven days, when in the midst of a heavenly light I saw Mary holding her divine Son in her arms. 'My daughter,' said she to me, 'three days more of prison, and after forty days, thou shalt leave this state of pain.'

"Such happy news renewed my courage to prepare for the frightful combat awaiting. The Queen of Heaven reminded me of the name I had received in Baptism, saying: 'Thou art Lumena, as thy Spouse is called Light, or Sun. Fear not. I will aid thee. Now nature, whose weakness asserts itself, is humbling thee. In the moment of struggle grace will come to thee to lend its force. The angel who is mine also, Gabriel, whose name expresses force, will come to thy succor. I will recommend thee especially to his care.' The vision disappeared, leaving my prison scented with a fragrance like incense. I experienced a joy out of this world, something indefinable.

"What the Queen of Angels had prepared me for was soon experienced. Diocletian, despairing of bending me, decided on public chastisement to offend my virtue. He condemned me to be stripped and scourged, like the Spouse I preferred to him. These were his horrifying words: 'Since she is not ashamed to prefer, to an emperor like me, a malefactor condemned to an infamous death by His own people, she deserves that my justice shall treat her as He was treated.'

"The prison guards hesitated to unclothe me entirely, but they did tie me to a column in the presence of the great men of the Court. They lashed me with violence, until I was bathed in blood. My whole body felt like one open wound, but I did not faint.

"The tyrant had me dragged back to the dungeon, expecting me to die. I hoped to join my heavenly Spouse. Two angels, shining with light, appeared to me in the darkness. They poured a soothing balm on my wounds, bestowing on me a vigor I did not have before the torture.

"When the emperor was informed of the change that had come over me, he had me brought before him. He viewed me with a greedy desire, and tried to persuade me that I owed my healing and regained vigor to Jupiter and another god, whom he, the emperor, had sent to me. He attempted to impress me with his belief that Jupiter desired me to be empress of Rome. Joining to these seductive words, promises of great honor, cooing the most flattering words, Diocletian tried to caress me. Fiendishly he attempted to complete the work of hell which he had begun.

"The Divine Spirit, to whom I am indebted for constancy in preserving my purity, seemed to fill me with light and knowledge. To all the proofs which I gave of the solidity of our faith, neither Diocletian nor his own courtiers could find an answer. Then the frenzied emperor dashed at me, commanding a guard to chain an anchor round my neck, and bury me deep in the waters of the Tiber.

"The order was executed. I was cast into the water, but God sent to me two angels, who unfastened the anchor. It fell into the river mud, where it remains, no doubt, to the present time. The angels transported me gently. In full view of the multitude upon the river bank I came back unharmed, not even wet, after being plunged with the heavy anchor.

"When a cry of joy rose from the watchers on the shore, and so many embraced Christianity by proclaiming their belief in my God, Diocletian attributed my preservation to secret magic.

"Then the emperor had me dragged through the streets of Rome and shot at with a shower of arrows. My blood flowed, but I did not faint. Diocletian thought I was dying and commanded the guards to carry me back to my dungeon. Heaven honored me with a new favor there. I fell into a sweet sleep. A second time the tyrant attempted to have me pierced with sharper darts. Again the archers bent their bows. They gathered all their strength, but the arrows refused to second their intentions. The emperor was present. In a rage, he called me a magician, and, thinking that the action of the fire could destroy the enchantment, he ordered the darts to be made red in a furnace, and directed against my heart. He was obeyed, but these darts, after having gone over a part of the space which they were to cross to come to me, took quite a contrary direction, and returned to strike those by whom they had been hurled. Six of the archers were killed by them. Several among them renounced paganism. The people began to render public testimony to the power of God that protected me. These murmurs and acclamations infuriated the tyrant.

"He determined to hasten my death by piercing my neck with a lance. My soul took flight toward my heavenly Spouse, who placed me, with the crown of virginity and the palm of martyrdom, in a distinguished place among the elect. The day that was so happy for me and saw me enter into glory was Friday, the third hour after midday, the same hour that saw my divine Master expire."

2. The Priest's Tale

Don Francesco narrates the second revelation as he heard it from a zealous priest who is convinced that he saw Philomena. The priest's experience as he told it at the shrine in the presence of the sacred relics of the Saint has been recorded. A résumé follows.

While walking through a country thicket a priest met a young girl. She stopped him to inquire if he really had a picture of St. Philomena in his church. Assured on that point, the girl asked what he knew about the Saint. In good faith, the priest answered that he knew only what he had heard from others about the inscription on the tombstone, and as simply as possible the priest explained to her the symbolic meaning.

The ladylike maiden listened patiently to the stories the priest told regarding the reports of wonderful happenings that were taking place daily at the Saint's shrine.

Then the girl told him she knew some facts regarding the life and martyrdom of the Saint. She clearly explained the reason for the cruel death Philomena had to undergo when the emperor tried to coerce her into a sinful marriage. Naturally Philomena loved her parents, and suffered keenly in the knowledge that she was refusing her father's wish when she rejected the hand of Diocletian. The alternative would be a cruel war, waged on her father's small Grecian state. But Philomena was motivated by the highest integrity. She could not and would not marry a man who at that moment was already married. Moreover, Philomena had vowed chastity to God. She had no desire to marry anyone, even to please her parents and save a kingdom.

Amazed by the girl's clarity and smoothness in telling the story, the priest interrupted her with questions. Where had she read that information? How did she know Philomena's parents were converted from paganism, and that Philomena had been baptized Christian at her birth?

In a tone of grave surprise, the maiden answered with a question. "Is it to me you point for the name of the book? As if I could be ignorant of the facts I tell you. No, surely, I do not deceive you. I know what I am saying. I am certain of it. Believe me."

The girl disappeared, leaving the priest mystified. Where had he seen a person who resembled her? Suddenly he realized. This girl was like the picture of St. Philomena. She was Philomena! The priest believed.

3. The Artisan's Tale

The narrative of the artisan follows along the same line, although he and the priest and the nun lived in distant parts of Italy, and were unknown to their families or to one another.

The artisan claims he saw Diocletian try to woo the virgin. When she repulsed him, the emperor flattered himself with his importance by a mere assurance that he would soon break the maiden. He tried to force her hand by threats, then actual torment. In a fit of rage the emperor ordered the girl's execution. Immediately he relented, because his maddened passions gored him on to make her his wife. But the virgin was dead.

The artisan is sure he heard the emperor cry out: "Woe is me! Philomena will never be my spouse! She has been refractory to my will to her last breath. Now she is dead. How shall I be able to live?" Then he tore his beard like an animal in a cage.

He seized on with his teeth whatever came in his way, screaming that he no longer desired to be ruler of Rome.

Public Attestation[78]

of the miraculous exudation of manna* from the statue of St. Philomena, virgin and martyr, on the eleventh of last August, 1823, in the church of Santa Maria delle Grazie, where rests the very body of the martyr, in Mugnano del Cardinale.

"We the undersigned pastor and priests in the locality of Mugnano del Cardinale, in the diocese of Nola, hereby testify as eyewitnesses, that on the eleventh of August, the day following the celebration, commemorating the translation of the body of Saint Philomena, Virgin and Martyr, which took place on the tenth of the said month, in the course of the Jubilee octave, and precisely on Monday (twenty-one o'clock), to the church of Santa Maria delle Grazie, where rests the body of the said Saint Philomena, and we noticed that till midnight the statue of the said martyr was copiously exuding a fluid of clear manna in the manner of natural perspiration coming in abundance from her face and neck. While this prodigy was noticed on the statue of Saint Philomena, the other statues in the Church of Santa Maria delle Grazie were examined, those of Our Lady of Grace, Saint Joseph, and also the marbles and the stuccos of the church, which were found to be dry, moistless, and dusty as were the other parts of the statue of Saint Philomena, namely, her feet, hands, forehead, and mantle, which were covered with the dust accumulated during the procession of the preceding day, which had taken place amid the scorching heat of the season and of a long dry spell. This exudation continued until late at night on Tuesday the 12th of the month, when the exudation ceased, but the liquid manna remained on the face and neck of the statue without drying up, until the octave of

[78] Don Francesco, p. 164.
*Here "manna" refers to a miraculous exudation of oil. —*Editor.*

the feast, which was on the 17th, observed and venerated by out-of-town people. In like manner, the wide, red silk ribbon on which is fastened the relic and which hangs around the neck of the statue, remains soaked and on the date given below, August 22, 1823, the exudation on it is still fresh, for it has not dried at all.

"Of all these happenings, we have been eyewitnesses, together with a great number of the inhabitants of our district and out-of-town people who had hastened here to observe the manifest prodigy.

"For the glory of God so marvelous in His saints, for the triumph of the Catholic Church, to the honor of the Holy Virgin and Martyr, Filomena, for the edification of the faithful, and for the everlasting remembrance of posterity, we have drawn up the present document under our hand and seal, and confirmed by the parochial seal, on this day, the 22nd of August of MDCCCXXIII."

Signatures: (eighteen)

> Don Giuseppe Rega — Pastor and Vicar
> Paolo Ippolito — Steward
> Domenico Tedeshi — Steward
> Gennaro Montuori — Priest
> Francesco Bianco — Spiritual Father of the Congregation
> Salvatore Barbato — Steward
> Liberato Rega — Priest
> Antonio Rega — Priest
> Giuseppe Serio — Priest (ex Augustinian)
> Pasquale Lopez — Priest
> Vincenzo Ippolito — Priest
> Saverio Bisesti — Priest
> Giovanni Canonico — Priest
> Don Orazio Cavaliere — Priest Confessor
> Don Domenico Montuori — Priest (ex Augustinian)
> Don Sabbato Masucci — Priest Confessor
> Don Pasquale Buccieri — Priest
> Don Francesco di Lucia — Priest Confessor

"We too, the undersigned, Mayor, Councilmen, and officials, of the locality of Mugnano and Cardinale (Mugnano del Cardinale is the full name of the locality), together with other citizens, attest (testify to) the public miracle of the emanation of manna from the statue of Saint Philomena, Virgin and Martyr, which took place on the eleventh of last August in the year 1823, in the village church of Santa Maria delle Grazie, where rests the very body and the phial of blood."

Don Mario Bisesti — Burgess
Don Gregorio Sirignano — First Elector
Paolo Bianco — Second Elector
Don Girolamo di Gennaro — Communal Chancellor
Don Giovanni Antonio Sirignano — Police Deputy
Notaro Don Gennaro di Gennaro — Councilman-notary
Felice Bianco
Don Domenico Guerriero
Michele Mauro
Ferdinando Montuori
Girolamo Giuliano
Nicola d'Andrea
Giovanni Masuccio
Don Raffaele Marano di Monteforte
Don Giovanbattista Bianco
D. Pasquale Vitale
Notaro Don Tommaso d'Andrea
Don Girolamo Bianco
Don Amato Bianco
Don Antonio Natale
Don Giovanni Bianco
Don Felice Ippolito
Don Mattia Tedeschi
Ludovico Napolitano
Salvatore Bianco
Carmine Montano
Pasquale Bianco

MRS. JAMESON'S LEGEND[79]

"In the year 1802, while some excavations were going forward in the catacomb of Priscilla at Rome, a sepulchre was discovered containing the skeleton of a young female; on the exterior were rudely painted some of the symbols constantly recurring in these chambers of the dead: an anchor, an olive branch (emblems of hope and peace), a scourge, two arrows, and a javelin: above them the following inscription, of which

[79] Mrs. Anna Brownell Jameson, *Sacred and Legendary Art,* 2 vols. (Boston: James R. Osgood & Co.), Vol. 2, pp. 287–289.

the beginning and end were destroyed: LUMENA PAX TE CUM FI. The remains, reasonably supposed to be those of one of the early martyrs for the faith, were sealed up and deposited in the treasury of relics in the Lateran; here they remained for some years unthought of. On the return of Pius VII from France, a Neapolitan prelate was sent to congratulate him. One of the priests in his train, who wished to create a sensation in the district, where the long residence of the French had probably caused some decay of piety, begged for a few relics to carry home, and these recently discovered remains were bestowed on him; the inscription was translated somewhat freely, to signify 'Santa Filumena, rest in peace. Amen.' Another priest, whose name is suppressed because of his great humility, was favored by a vision in the broad noonday, in which he beheld the glorious virgin Filomena, who was pleased to reveal to him that she had suffered death for preferring the Christian faith and her vow of chastity to the addresses of the emperor, who wished to make her his wife.

"This vision leaving much of her history obscure, a certain young artist, whose name is also suppressed, perhaps because of his great humility, was informed in a vision that the emperor alluded to was Diocletian, and at the same time the torments and persecutions suffered by the Christian virgin Filomena, as well as her wonderful constancy, were also revealed to him. There were some difficulties in the way of the Emperor Diocletian, which incline the writer of the historical account to the opinion that the young artist in his vision may have made a mistake, and the emperor may have been, not Diocletian, but Maximian. The facts, however, now admitted of no doubt: the relics were carried by the priest Francesco di Lucia to Naples; they were enclosed in a case of wood resembling in form the human body; this figure was habited in a petticoat of white satin, and over it a crimson tunic after the Greek fashion; the face was painted to represent nature, a garland of flowers was placed on the head, and in the hands a lily and a javelin with the point reversed to express her purity and martyrdom;

then she was laid in a half-sitting posture in a sarcophagus, of which the sides were glass; and after lying for some time in state in the chapel of the Terres family in the church of Sant' Angiolo, she was carried in grand procession to Mugnano, a little town about twenty miles from Naples, amid the acclamations of the people, working many and surprising miracles by the way.

"Such is the legend of St. Filomena, and such the authority on which she has become within the last twenty years one of the most popular saints in Italy. Jewels to the value of many thousand crowns have been offered at her shrine, and solemnly placed round the neck of her image or suspended to her girdle. I found effigy in the Venetian churches, and in those of Bologna and Lombardy. Her worship has extended to enlightened Tuscany. At Pisa the church of San Francesco contains a chapel dedicated lately to Santa Filomena; over the altar is a picture by Sabatelli representing the saint as a beautiful nymph-like figure floating down from heaven, attended by two angels bearing the lily, palm, and javelin, and beneath in the foreground the sick and maimed who are healed by her intercession; round the chapel are suspended hundreds of votive offerings, displaying the power and popularity of the saint. There is also a graceful German print after Fürich, representing her in the same attitude in which the image lies in the shrine. I did not expect to encounter St. Filomena at Paris; but to my surprise, I found a chapel dedicated to her in the church of St. Gervais; a statue of her with the flowers, the dart, the scourge, and the anchor under her feet; and two pictures, one surrounded, after the antique fashion, with scenes of her life. In the church of Saint-Merry, at Paris, there is a chapel recently dedicated to 'Ste Philomene,' the walls covered with a series of frescos from her legend, painted by Amaury Duval — a very fair imitation of the old Italian style.

"I have heard that St. Filomena is patronized by the Jesuits; even so, it is difficult to account for the extension and popularity of her story in this nineteenth century."

Father Chandlery's Version[80]

"In the Pontificate of Pius VII a remarkable slab attracted the attention of the custodians of this catacomb [of St. Priscilla] who were then prosecuting investigations, and on May 25, 1802, the tomb was formally examined. On the tiles that enclosed it was the following inscription: 'Philomena Pax Tecum.' The devices accompanying these simple words — an anchor, an arrow, and a palm — determined the spot as the last resting-place of a martyr.

"The tomb was opened by Monsignor Ludovici, who disclosed the precious remains to the gaze of the assistants and bystanders. Beside them stood the phial containing the blood of the Saint. From an examination of the relics it was ascertained that Philomena had been martyred in her tender youth, at about twelve or thirteen years of age. In 1805, the relics were translated to Mugnano, near Naples. Blessed John Vianney, Curé d' Ars, had a great devotion to this Saint."

Dr. Brewer's Version[81]*

In Brewer's *A Dictionary of Miracles* the name Philomena is also spelled with an "F" — "Filumena." The account reads: "The existence of this person was wholly unknown till three tiles were discovered, in 1802, in the cemetery of St. Priscilla. Her ghost revealed her antecedents. Her body was removed to Naples in 1805, and was honoured by so many miracles that she was called 'The Thaumaturgist of the Nineteenth Century.' In 1852 Pius IX granted great indulgences to those who honoured this new saint."

Under the caption: "Saint Filumena, a Nineteenth Century Saint Asserts Herself," the Reverend Dr. Brewer continues:

[80] Peter J. Chandlery, S.J., *Pilgrim Walks in Rome* (London: Manresa Press, 1908), pp. 410–411.

[81] E. Cobham Brewer, *A Dictionary of Miracles* (Philadelphia: J. B. Lippincott Co., 1884), pp. xxxiii, 22, 476.

*The reader should be alerted that Dr. Brewer's extremely erudite book, though it quotes virtually entirely from authoritative Catholic sources and is a goldmine of valuable information, was nonetheless written purposely to scoff at Catholic "credulity" with regard to the miracles of the saints. —*Editor.*

". . . The virgin martyr herself told a priest and a nun so in a dream. She told them she was called 'Filumena' because she was 'Fi/lia/ Lumena,' the daughter of the 'Light of the World.' In confirmation of this revelation, when the bones were carried to Mugnano, the saint repaired her own skeleton, made her hair grow, and performed so many other miracles, that those who doubt the statement of the 'virgin martyr' would not be convinced even if they themselves had dreamt the dream."

In a chronological arrangement of *Thaumaturgists,* Brewer tells the "Marvelous Story of Filumena, the Nineteenth Century Thaumaturgist," who, according to this prolific writer, was martyred in the third century A.D.

St. Philomena in 1950

Information here released is dated November 18, 1950. These authentic answers received from Monsignor Vincenzo Malasomma, rector of the minor seminary in Naples, verify other material in this book.

"1. The colors of the garments covering the mortal remains of Saint Philomena are three: White, red, and light blue.

    a) The tunic is white, richly embroidered in gold.

    b) Over the tunic there is a stole of a purple red, and it, too, is richly embroidered.

    c) The mantle is sky-blue.

"2. In Mugnano there is a wooden statue, which is exposed during the novena of the feast in August and carried in procession. During the rest of the year this statue is kept in the *Sala del Tesoro* (the Treasure Hall). Saint Philomena's body, clothed in the garments described above, rests on the second altar to the left of one who enters the shrine. The bones have been gracefully and artistically encased (in a lifelike human form), and so the onlooker gets the impression of being in the presence of a young girl peacefully resting. Her face, which in (the course of) time has changed its position, is (made) of wax.

"3. The phial in which this martyr's blood was preserved was found broken. The blood adhering to the glass was scraped off and put into a costly reliquary.

"Looking at it (the blood in congealed particles), one has the impression of looking at tiny precious stones. According to the statements of reliable persons, the brightness of these particles of blood varies with the circumstances.

"(Is there any) effusion? There has been a confusion. Upon unearthing the body of this great Virgin and Martyr, the broken phial was found and the dried up blood flowed (spilled) out.

"Being that it is almost certain that the body of the Saint was laid into the loculus a considerable time after her death, this effusion cannot but be miraculous. Since that blood had flowed out (spilled out) of the phial, it must have been in a liquid state (at the time), though at a remarkable distance from the time of the Saint's death.

"To speak of the *first* or *last* miracle of Saint Philomena is an impossible undertaking. *The miracles are so numerous, that they cannot be counted.* Up to 1861, the chronicles are full of great and clamorous miracles. Since 1861, the year in which the shrine was taken over by the secular authorities, no one took care to hand down to posterity a chronicle of the shrine. Nevertheless there have been miracles even at this time."

St. Philomena Today

The following is taken from a letter written by the rector of the sanctuary of St. Philomena, Monsignor Luigi Ezposito, Mugnano del Cardinale, Avellino, Naples, in February, 1951.

"In the Sanctuary of Saint Philomena we conserve the body of the Saint above an altar called 'The Tomb.' What is left of the body was encased in a statue of papier-mâché. This statue was stately dressed in rich clothing embroidered in gold. The white tunic underneath is likewise gold embroidered. Around the shoulders of the Saint are two magnificent cloaks, artistically arranged. The one garment is purple-red. Over this stole is the azure mantle.

"The head of the statue is also made of papier-mâché. At first the face was designed in wax. Fearing that wax would soon change its color, the image maker substituted papier-mâché, the colors of which are more resistant to the influence of light.

"In the course of time the body of the Saint has frequently moved itself. Factually: We had many motions of the Saint. The last one which occurred in 1907 in the presence of a pilgrimage coming from Piedimonte d'Alife, a town of 5,000 inhabitants, near Benevento, has been canonically stated by the Bishop of Nola, Monsignor Agnello Renzullo. He stated the fact after having interrogated the Sisters of the Sanctuary, and the sacristans of the Church, and after having got a citation from the Chancery of the Bishop of Alife who had questioned the pilgrims of his diocese.

"Two years ago there was another movement by which the left ear (of the image) which was until then invisible, became perfectly visible. Before this time the very existence of this ear was even unknown.

"Moreover we have a magnificent statue carved in wood, which is exposed to the veneration of the faithful on her feast in August. This is the statue that gave forth manna in the presence of the people. Of this fact there exists a declaration signed by the clergy of the Church and the civil and military authorities of the place.

"To speak of (recent) miracles is not an easy matter, because they are very *numerous*. Canonical investigation was never made about them (*the Saint has been canonized since 1837*)."

If you have enjoyed this book, consider making your next selection from among the following . . .

At your bookdealer or direct from the publisher.

Prices guaranteed through June 30, 1989.